WELL
DONE

WELL DONE

DONE

GOOD AND FAITHFUL SERVANT

Fulfilling Your Purpose
in the Harvest

Steven J. Campbell

Well Done: Good and Faithful Servant

© 2013 by Steven J. Campbell

Author grants permission for any non-commercial reproduction to promote the Kingdom of God.

All other rights reserved.

ISBN-13: 978-0615808444

ISBN-10: 0615808441

Revised Printing—October 2019

Cover image and design by:

Alex B. Campbell
        and
Austin J. Campbell

Table of Contents

Introduction

You can hear, "Well done, good and faithful servant" since it is available to whoever is willing. If you are that willing one, then you will do what it takes to hear those words directly from Jesus. The key to hearing those words is not in striving to hear them; it is in seeking to know Jesus and to please Him.

In reading this book, you will be challenged and encouraged as I have been in writing it. Throughout its pages, you will find encouragement as well as exhortations. We need both the exhortations and the encouragements.

Jesus was both an encourager and an exhorter. We see this as He spoke to the seven churches in Revelation chapters two and three. He exhorted them and encouraged them. I have tried to follow the same pattern in this book—to exhort and to encourage.

In writing this book, my heart was to be like Jesus who is full of grace and truth. Grace is not grace if it is not full of truth, and truth is not truth unless it is full of grace. However, since we all see in part and know in part, I know I have not written with perfect grace and truth. Still, know that it was my desire to be both gracious and truthful with you, the reader.

The main purpose in writing this book is to stir-up hope within you, hope that propels you to embrace the cost of your destiny—being a disciplined follower of Jesus.

Great hope enables great sacrifice. Jesus endured the cross with great hope knowing His sacrifice would produce a great harvest. The same is true for you as you embrace the cross and follow Jesus; you will have great hope of fulfilling your purpose in the end-time harvest and of hearing, ***"Well done, good and faithful servant. Enter into the joy of your Lord."***

Part One:

THE
HARVEST

Chapter 1

Words

There are words that we all long to hear—words creating a feeling within us of our worth, showing us we are valuable. Jesus, the Word made flesh, is the greatest communicator of our value. He said God loved us so much that, *"He gave His only begotten Son, that whoever believes in Him should not perish but have everlasting life" (John 3:16).*

Now, that is immeasurable value—God giving His only Son for you! Jesus' death on the cross shows *God's* perception of your value; He thinks you are worth the death of His only Son! Wow, just think on that! You are valuable beyond your current comprehension, beyond your wildest imagination.

The Power of Words

The Bible does not agree with the children's rhyme that says, "Sticks and stones may break my bones, but words can't hurt me." The Bible shows just the opposite; it shows words are powerful.

Jesus, knowing the power of our words, informs us that what we say is a serious matter. He does not take lightly what we say to others or what they say to us.

"Carelessly call a brother 'idiot!' and you just might find yourself hauled into court. Thoughtlessly yell 'stupid!' at a sister and you are on the brink of hellfire. The

simple moral fact is that words kill."
(Matthew 5:22 TMSG)

Jesus says words can hurt; therefore, we are accountable for what we speak to others. Moreover, if we remember we have hurt someone with our words, we need to make it right.

Jesus also reminds us that we will give an account for all our careless words. He says, *"I can guarantee that on judgment day people will have to give an account of every careless word they say" (Matthew 12:36 GW).* Through the teachings of Jesus, we understand that words have great power.

Words can create. God's spoken words created the heavens and the earth and also create us anew—we are born again by His words. *For you have been born again, not of perishable seed, but of imperishable, through the living and enduring word of God. (1 Peter 1:23 NIV)*

The most powerful words that we will ever experience are the words that God speaks over us because what He speaks about us has eternal consequences.

The Words We Long to Hear

We all long to know we accomplished our purpose in life—that our life was not wasted, but had real meaning and true purpose. Since God knows all He purposed for our lives, only He can give an accurate assessment of our lives. Therefore, the words we all long to hear from Him are, *"Well done, good and faithful servant."*

If you stand before God and hear those words, it will be worth any price paid to follow Him. To please the God of the universe, the creator of all things, is of more value than you can comprehend at this time. When you please God with your life, you will feel incomprehensible value and experience a joy unspeakable when He pronounces His verdict on how you lived. Jesus gives a parable showing this in Matthew 25:14–23:

> *For the kingdom of heaven is like a man traveling to a far country, who called his own servants and delivered his goods to them. And to one he gave five talents, to another two, and to another one, to each according to his own ability; and immediately he went on a journey. . . . he who had received five talents . . . His lord said to him, "Well done, good and faithful servant; you were faithful over a few things . . . Enter into the joy of your lord." . . . He also who had received two talents . . . His lord said to him, "Well done, good and faithful servant; you were faithful over a few things . . . Enter into the joy of your lord."*

A talent in Jesus' time was a very valuable sum of money (about two years' wages). Today we think of a "talent" as our gifting or opportunity to serve God. In the parable, Jesus shows us that we all have talents to use in our lives as we see fit. We can either invest our gifting in the kingdom or waste it. If we want God to say to us, *"Well done, good and faithful servant,"* we must invest wisely into His kingdom.

This is such a serious matter with God that we see He will severely judge one that is unfaithful with his "talent"—did not use his life's opportunities for the kingdom. In fact, Jesus pronounces that person "wicked and lazy" and he/she will be cast into outer darkness— *"You wicked and lazy servant . . . cast the unprofitable servant into the outer darkness" (Matthew 25:26, 30).* What a contrast—joy unspeakable or torment beyond belief—depending upon what they with their "talent."

Why was this servant "wicked and lazy"? Because he had no true relationship with his lord. He did not know his lord as a master full of love. Furthermore, he was a coward. One rendering of Matthew 5:24–30 says:

The servant given one thousand said, "Master, I know you have high standards and hate careless ways, that you demand the best and make no allowances for error. I was afraid I might disappoint you, so I found a good hiding place and secured your money. Here it is, safe and sound down to the last cent."

The master was furious. "That's a terrible way to live! It's criminal to live cautiously like that! If you knew I was after the best, why did you do less than the least? The least you could have done would have been to invest the sum with the bankers, where at least I would have gotten a little interest.

"Take the thousand and give it to the one who risked the most. And get rid of this "play-it-safe" who won't go out on a limb. Throw him out into utter darkness." (TMSG)

No doubt, this is the reason many do not use their "talent" for the kingdom; they want to "play-it-safe" instead of stepping out into their purpose by faith. However, God does not like us being cowardly, not using our faith.

Be courageous because your life after death is eternal, whereas life in this world is temporary. Live your life for eternal rewards, not worldly rewards, since eternal things are much more valuable than worldly things. In fact, your eternal rewards will be determined by how you lived your life in this world.

Hidden Talents

We all have or have had "hidden talents." There are two forms of these hidden talents; talents you don't see in yourself and talents others don't see in you.

1. Talents hidden from yourself.
   You have talents that you are not aware of; it takes other people to see the talents you have. These are talents you do not see in yourself but others see them in you.

2. Talents you hide from others.
   These are talents you know you have, but you do not use them; you hide them. Why? Usually because of fear of what others would think or say.

The parable we just discussed shows what Jesus thinks of that behavior—He does not want you hiding any of your talents He gave you.

The Good News

The gospel of the kingdom is good news ("gospel" means *good news*). The good news is that God works in us to do His will, to be what He wants us to be.

Jesus did not leave us as orphans when He went back to heaven but sent the Holy Spirit as our Helper (see John 14:16–18). The Holy Spirit helps us to be good and faithful servants.

When Jesus proclaimed the Holy Spirit as our "Helper," it means He helps us to will and to do what we need to do. Philippians 2:13 confirms this: ***"For it is God who works in you both to will and to do for His good pleasure."***

Additionally, Jesus said He would never leave us nor forsake us; therefore we can boldly proclaim He is our helper and we will not be afraid—even of not being a good and faithful servant. Hebrews 13:5–6 states:

> ***Since God assured us, "I'll never let you down, never walk off and leave you," we can boldly quote,***
>
> ***God is there, ready to help;***
> ***I'm fearless no matter what.***
> ***Who or what can get to me? (TMSG)***

We can do all things through the strength of Jesus Christ (Philippians 4:13). He strengthens us to do His will, providing everything we need from His riches in glory (Philippians 4:19). We can be good and faithful servants.

The entire gospel is good news, including the Scriptures describing wicked servants and their ends. Yes, the news of the unprofitable and the cowardly being cast out is good news (but not for them). Why? Because if everyone is treated the same no matter what they did in their life, then good deeds would have no meaning or value. The good news is that Jesus makes a distinction between profitable servants and those that are not. Since God makes such serious distinctions between those that do right and those that do wrong, it magnifies the value of doing what pleases God.

Whatever we become, we become by the grace of God, not by our power or our might but by His Spirit (Zechariah 4:6).

> *But by the grace of God I am what I am, and His grace toward me was not in vain; but I labored more abundantly than they all, yet not I, but the grace of God which was with me. (1 Corinthians 15:10)*

We are empowered by His grace for a purpose. We are not to receive this grace in vain—to waste His grace by not working with it. Paul knew he was what he was by God's grace, which means he had the responsibility to labor with the grace given to him. Paul had an *abundance* of grace given to him; therefore, he was expected to labor more abundantly.

If we do not use what God has given us then we have received our talent in vain. Remember, Jesus called the one not using what God gave him "wicked and lazy."

Even so, we have God at work in us so we can choose to overcome laziness and be a faithful servant using our talents.

Looking for His Son

When we stand before God one day, how will we ensure we hear, *"Well done"*? It will be by knowing what God is looking for.

In the beginning, the purpose of God was to create humanity in His image—He was looking for His likeness in Adam and Eve. As we know, they sinned and fell short of His glory. Since then, all humans have sinned and fallen short of His glory (Romans 3:23). However, if anyone is in Christ, he is a new creation with all things becoming new. In Christ Jesus, we have the glory of God again (see John 17:22).

The first thing God looks for in us is the glory of His Son. Jesus in us is the hope of glory (Colossians 1:27). We will hear *"Well done"* if God sees Jesus' image in us. From the beginning to the end, it has always been God's purpose to see His image in us. Even so, we can rest in the fact of Jesus being the author and finisher of our faith—He is the One producing His image in us.

The focus of our life should be to become like Jesus. The central characteristic of Jesus is love. If we have learned to love then we will be bearing the image of God, for God is love. To be like Jesus, our greatest duty is to love as He loves. Since Jesus expresses His love by works of love, our love will also produce works of love. He will work His image in us so we will have those works of love. How does He do this? He does it through Jesus.

For we are His workmanship, created in Christ Jesus for good works, which God prepared beforehand that we should walk in them. (Ephesians 2:10)

God is looking for our Christlikeness—seeing if we are doing what Jesus did with the same attitude of love. In 1 Corinthians 13 we see the importance of love motivating our actions—for we can have all faith and still not be like Christ if we do not have love. Our works come from the motivation of our hearts. If our hearts are bad, then our works are bad. Jesus lets us know that "good works" from a heart that does not love God and others is not acceptable to Him (see Matthew 7:21–23). God looks at what we do to see if it is through Christlikeness. If it is through a Christlike attitude, then it is a good work. Good works only come from a heart of love for God and a love for others.

Christlike Works

In Christ we are a new creation, all things become new. Because of this, God gives us the same ministry that Jesus has—to do the same works. Jesus assures us of this when He says:

"Most assuredly, I say to you, he who believes in Me, the works that I do he will do also; and greater works than these he will do, because I go to My Father." (John 14:12)

The key to doing the works of Jesus and even greater works is "he who believes in Me." This is not "head-believing" but "heart-believing." In your heart, you believe in Jesus' power within you. Believing in Jesus in your heart is the birthplace for His works and even greater works.

Jesus cursed a fig tree and it quickly withered away. He used this to show about the greater works that we will do.

> *". . . Assuredly, I say to you, if you have faith and do not doubt, you will not only do what was done to the fig tree, but also if you say to this mountain, 'Be removed and be cast into the sea,' it will be done.'" (Matthew 21:21)*

Mark 11:23 declares:

> *"For assuredly, I say to you, whoever says to this mountain, 'Be removed and be cast into the sea,' and does not doubt in his heart, but believes that those things he says will be done, he will have whatever he says.'"*

Jesus is speaking of a literal mountain—"this mountain." Then He speaks of casting a literal tree into the sea:

> *". . . If you have faith as a grain of mustard seed, you can say to this mulberry tree, 'Be pulled up by the roots and be planted in the sea,' and it would obey you." (Luke 17:6)*

Why did Jesus choose these types of greater works for us to do? First, it is to show the power of our words when we speak in faith. Second, it is to show Jesus has authority over every natural law. To pluck up a tree by its roots and have it planted in the sea simply by commanding it is impossible. Also, to move a mountain into the sea simply by commanding it is impossible. But *nothing* is impossible with God! These works will show what Jesus has declared, ***"With men it is impossible, but not with God; for with God all things are possible" (Mark 10:27).***

Why have these things not happened yet? This type of faith will not come apart from God clearly showing it is His will at that moment. Remember, Jesus never did these things even though He had the faith to do them because He only did what He saw the Father doing. Even so, there will be a time when we are instructed to do these things, proving Jesus' words are true. Yes, we have that kind of power in our words when *He* directs us to speak to the literal mountain—if we believe *in Him.*

Certainly, it is amazing to think we will do the same works as Jesus. Even more amazing is the fact that Jesus assures us we will do even greater works. No doubt, this is why He started His proclamation with "Most assuredly." When Jesus says something so forcefully, it is because we need to be impacted by the weight of His words. Even heaven and earth will pass away, but His words will not fail—they are a sure thing. Surely it will take place exactly as He proclaimed; to believe otherwise is pride—thinking we know more than God.

Humility believes what God says—that we *will* do the same works of Jesus and even greater. Pride believes something other than what God says and God resists the proud, but He gives grace to the humble. Believe what

God says, for without faith it is impossible to please Him (Hebrews 11:6).

Christlikeness and the Harvest

God made us ambassadors for Christ. An ambassador is an official representative, in this case, of Jesus. We are to carry out the ministry of Jesus on the earth, but we cannot do this apart from being in Christ. In Christ, we become a completely new creation; then we are given the same ministry as Jesus—the ministry of reconciliation.

> *Therefore, if anyone is in Christ, he is a new creation; old things have passed away; behold, all things have become new. Now all things are of God, who has reconciled us to Himself through Jesus Christ, and has given us the ministry of reconciliation, that is, that God was in Christ reconciling the world to Himself, not imputing their trespasses to them, and has committed to us the word of reconciliation.*
>
> *Now then, we are ambassadors for Christ, as though God were pleading through us: we implore you on Christ's behalf, be reconciled to God. (2 Corinthians 5:17–20)*

God gives our words power to reconcile others to Him. These are the days of salvation and God has called us to use our talents in the harvest.

> *... I tell you, now is the time of God's favor, now is the day of salvation.*
> *(2 Corinthians 6:2 NIV)*

God's grace enables us to use our talents wisely in His kingdom. Because of this, we can be a productive servant with the grace He gives us. This brings us to the main theme of this book: fulfilling our part of the ministry of reconciliation (bringing in the harvest) and hearing God say, *"Well done, good and faithful servant."*

Remember, you are unique; no one else can be you. No one else can do all you can do. Be who you are by releasing all your talents. Be unique!

Chapter 2

What Is the Harvest?

The ministry of reconciliation, seeing people born again, is the central part of the harvest. Even so, it is just a part of the harvest. There is more to the harvest than many realize; with that in mind, we will explore some other aspects of the harvest in this chapter. Each aspect of the harvest could become a book in itself, but I will only cover these topics in a brief manner.

The History of Harvest

In the beginning God created the harvest (see Genesis 1:11–12). He even made a covenant in Genesis 8:22 with His creation that it will last as long as the earth lasts:

> *While the earth remains,*
> *Seedtime and harvest . . .*
> *Shall not cease.*

The history of the harvest is from the beginning days of the earth and lasting as long as the earth remains. Adam and Eve harvested seed-bearing plants and fruit trees for their food. Today, we still harvest the same items for food as well as many other items. Harvesting is part of the natural order of the earth; plus, the earth also has the spiritual to be harvested.

Natural and Spiritual Harvest

There is a spiritual harvest and there is a natural harvest. But before we go any further, we need to understand what the word "harvest" means. The word has several related meanings. The following is my oversimplified definition of this word. The word "harvest" means: *to gather or to get what is mature.*

To understand the spiritual harvest, we first need to have some understanding of the natural harvest. Examples of natural harvesting are: a farmer gathering his crop, a hunter getting his game, or a person catching fish. All these obtain their harvest for sustaining life by severing something from its life. This shows us the underlying meaning of the word "harvest" in the Hebrew language— *severed.*

Harvesting is removing something from its environment of life: a fish from water, a plant from the ground, a fruit from the tree, wildlife from nature, and so on. The basic reason for harvesting is to sustain life. An example: a vegetable severed from life (the ground) sustains life in the person who eats it.

To be involved in the *spiritual* harvest is to help sever someone from a life of sin and death into a new life. Jesus called it being "born again." When you were physically born, the umbilical cord was severed; when you were spiritually born (born again), the old life of sin was severed. The Scriptures declare that you are in Christ when you are born again—severed from the old life, born into the new life (Jesus). In Christ, you have new life!

Your physical life started when you were within your mother; your spiritual life starts when you are in Jesus Christ.

. . . if anyone is in Christ, he is a new creation. Old things have disappeared, and—look!—all things have become new! (2 Corinthians 5:17 ISV)

Discipleship

Although the central part of the harvest is leading people to Jesus, it does not stop there. Being born again is only the beginning of our life in Christ. After that we are to become Jesus' disciples.

"All authority in heaven and on earth has been given to me. So wherever you go, make disciples of all nations: Baptize them in the name of the Father, and of the Son, and of the Holy Spirit. Teach them to do everything I have commanded you." (Matthew 28:18–20 GW)

We are not to just make converts; we are to make disciples. To be born again is the first step in becoming a disciple. The next step is being trained in the teachings of Jesus and following them. The word "disciple" could be translated as "a disciplined follower." Thus, a disciple is a disciplined follower of Jesus and His teachings.

Even so, a disciple is not just following a set of teachings; he is following a Person out the love for Him. A disciple will obey Jesus' teachings because he loves Him. And since he loves Him, he will also love His teachings. His teachings cannot be separated from Him—Jesus *is* what He taught.

The religious rulers of Jesus' time followed the commandments of God, but their heart was far from Him. Jesus wants us to follow Him by following His commandments from a heart of love. He said, *"If you love me, keep My commandments" (John 14:15).*

The Disciple's Worldview

A disciple of Jesus will have a worldview corresponding to Jesus' worldview. This will not occur immediately after being born again since we mature into Jesus' worldview as we grow in our knowledge of Him and follow His teachings. Only then will we increasingly view the world as Jesus views it and live in it as He did.

Disciples are the "light of the world." They stand out in the world like lights in the night even as Jesus stood out as The Great Light forever changing mankind. His followers change the world with their light by "enlightening" others with the life and teachings of Jesus. They proclaim the Biblical worldview and live by it.

The Word and the Spirit

Jesus is no longer on the earth, so how do we follow Him? We follow Him by following the example He set and His teachings. But how do we know what Jesus taught and how He lived on earth? First, we know how Jesus lived because the Bible tells us about Him and we follow Him through the Scriptures.

All Scripture is God-breathed and is useful for teaching, rebuking, correcting and training in righteousness, so that the man of God may be thoroughly equipped for every good work. (2 Timothy 3:16–17 NIV)

Second, when Jesus left earth, He did not leave us as orphans; He sent the Holy Spirit. The Holy Spirit reminds us of all Jesus taught so that we can follow His teachings.

"However, the helper, the Holy Spirit, whom the Father will send in my name, will teach you everything. He will remind you of everything that I have ever told you." (John 14:26 GW)

The Holy Spirit is our helper in understanding the Scriptures. Without the help of the Holy Spirit, we will be like the religious leaders of Jesus' day; they knew the teachings of Scripture but did not recognize the One the Scriptures pointed to—Jesus. They rejected Jesus because they did not correctly understand the Scriptures.

Third, we are not following someone who is dead. We are following the living Christ. If we are a disciple, then we live, move, and have our being in Him (Acts 17:28). He is the focus of our life. We do what we do based upon what we see Him doing. (We live like the catchphrase from a few years ago, "What would Jesus do?") Doing what Jesus would do is written on the heart of a disciple. They are not following a dead Christ from their head, but a living Christ from their heart.

The Mature

Harvesting is for that which is mature. The spiritual harvest includes everything that comes to maturity, including sin and evil as well as the good and righteous. Saints and sinners come to maturity. We need to comprehend this to understand the times we are living in. We are in the time of Isaiah chapter 60, which shows us the great contrast between the maturing of the harvests—the great light and the great darkness. Sin and darkness come to maturity at the same time as the light comes to maturity.

> *Arise, shine;*
> *For your light has come!*
> *And the glory of the LORD is risen upon*
> *   you.*
> *For behold, the darkness shall cover the*
> *   earth,*
> *And deep darkness the people;*
> *But the LORD will arise over you,*
> *And His glory will be seen upon you.*
> *The Gentiles shall come to your light,*
> *And kings to the brightness of your rising.*
> *   (Isaiah 60:1–3)*

The spiritual harvest is the maturing of both the wicked and the righteous as Jesus told us in the parable concerning the wheat and the weeds. At the time of the harvest both are gathered.

> *. . . The servants said to him, "Then do you want us to go and pull them out?" He said, "No, for if you pull out the weeds, you might pull out the wheat with them. Let both grow together until the harvest, and at harvest time I will tell the reapers, 'Gather the weeds first and tie them in*

bundles for burning, but bring the wheat into my barn.'" (Matthew 13:28–30 ISV)

This parable shows us the "weeds" (those not born again) will be "bundled for burning" (cast into the lake of fire—hell) and those who are born again are brought "into my barn" (heaven).

When is this harvest time that Jesus spoke of? Are we living in the time of the harvest? The next chapter will answer these important questions.

Chapter 3

When Is the Harvest?

From the beginning of time there has always been a harvest. In John 4:34–38, Jesus tells us the harvest is not for a future time—it is at hand. That was two-thousand years ago. There was a harvest then, and there is always a harvest in the now. However, Jesus speaks of a particular harvest that is the end of the age. In this chapter, we will look at the timing of this harvest—the end-time harvest.

The End-Time Harvest

The end-time harvest is the harvest taking place at the end of the age. The "end of the age" is when all things are matured. Jesus said, *"The harvest __is__ the end of the age" (Matthew 13:39).*

When Is the End of the Age?

The "end of the age" is when the time ends for this age. Jesus speaks of this time in Luke 21:20–32:

> *But when you see Jerusalem surrounded by armies, then know that its desolation is near. (Verse 20)*
>
> *And they will fall by the edge of the sword, and be led away captive into all nations. And Jerusalem will be trampled by Gentiles until the times of the Gentiles are fulfilled. (Verse 24)*

***So you also, when you see these things
happening, know that the kingdom of God
is near. Assuredly, I say to you, this
generation will by no means pass away
till all things take place. (Verses 31–32)***

The "end of the age" is not a day; it is a period of time.
This period is less than a generation, since that
generation will not disappear before all things take place
(Luke 21:32). What generation would this be? It is the
generation that sees Jerusalem restored to the Jewish
people (Luke 21:24). In 1967, after about two-thousand
years, Jerusalem came back into the hands of the Jews. If
this is what Jesus is speaking of in the above verses, then
the end of the age is the time of the generation alive in
1967 which will not die off before all things take place.
*However, 1967 may not be what Jesus is speaking of
here since the Temple Mount is still in dispute;* even so,
most of Jerusalem is in the hands of the Jews. At the
least, I believe we can say we are now living in the end-
time era.

If Jesus is speaking of the events of 1967, then at least
one person that was alive in 1967 will not die before all
things take place. Otherwise, the generation that Jesus
speaks of would have passed away and Jesus says that
that will not happen (Luke 21:32).

How long do people live now? Several live over one-
hundred years. Many believe mankind's life span is
limited to 120 years now (see Genesis 6:3). Does that
mean we have about 120 years after 1967 before the end
of this era? Possibly. It may be over 120 years or it may
be fewer than 120 years before the end of the age **IF**

Jesus is speaking of the events of 1967 especially considering the Scripture in Matthew 24:22:

> *"And unless those days were shortened, no flesh would be saved; but for the elect's sake those days will be shortened."*

However, it could easily be two-hundred years or more especially if we consider traditional Jewish thought. Many consider 7000 years as the time given for man on the earth. The Jewish year 6000 would be the year of the Messiah (what we would call the millennium—the 1000-year reign of Christ on the earth). In the year 2020, the Hebrew year will be 5780. Therefore, in Jewish thought we would have about 220 years before the end of this age and the beginning of the millennial reign of Christ. However, since Jesus said the days would be shortened, we cannot fix a date for the end of this age—*only* the Father knows the day and hour (see Mark 13:32).

Proclaiming the Kingdom

We are in the end-time era and there cannot be many more decades left to accomplish what Jesus says must take place before the end of this age:

> *All during this time, the good news—the Message of the kingdom—will be preached all over the world, a witness staked out in every country. And then the end will come. (Matthew 24:14 TMSG)*

The end-time gospel is the message of the kingdom. The message of the kingdom is:

1. Jesus is King.
2. He is coming to earth again.
3. He is coming to set up His kingship on the earth.
4. We will reign and rule with Jesus.
5. He will judge all things by His word.
6. The earth will be restored to its original glory and even greater.
7. It is time to prepare the way for The King.
8. Repent for the kingdom of heaven is at hand.
9. Seek first the kingdom of God and His righteousness.
10. Do not fear, for it is the Father's good pleasure to give you the kingdom.

(The above list is but a summary of the message of the kingdom, not a complete list.)

Prepare the Way

These are the days of preparing the way for The King to come to earth. We do this first by becoming a disciple. Then we proclaim the message of the kingdom, making disciples of all nations and teaching them to do all Jesus commanded (Matthew 28:19–20). When we have accomplished this, the end of this age will come.

Knowing the Time

Again, no one knows the day or hour of the end of this era. *"No one knows when that day or hour will come—not the angels in heaven, nor the Son, but only the Father" (Matthew 24:36 ISV).*

We cannot know the day or hour, but we should know when we are in the end-time season.

> *Then Jesus used this story as an illustration. "Look at the fig tree or any other tree. As soon as leaves grow on them, you know without being told that summer is near. In the same way, when you see these things happen, you know that the kingdom of God is near. I can guarantee this truth: This generation will not disappear until all this takes place."*
> *(Luke 21:29–32 GW)*

We know we are living in the end-time era because we see the "leaves coming on the trees"—especially the reality of Jerusalem being restored to the Jewish people in 1967.

The good news is that this is the end of one age and the beginning of another age with Jesus reigning as King. Preaching this good news brings forth a great hope and a great harvest.

When the good news of the kingdom is preached in the whole world, it produces the full end-time harvest—which is massive. We will discuss the size of this harvest in the next chapter.

Chapter 4

The Size of the Harvest

The statement, "God is more interested in quality than quantity" has its merits when speaking of converts verses disciples, but it falls short in proclaiming God's desire for all people to be saved. In fact, it may be interpreted as God not being concerned about every human being. However, 1 Timothy 2:3–4 says God wants all to be saved (quantity) and come to a knowledge of the truth (quality).

Filling the Earth

When God created the creatures of the sea and the birds of the air, He said, *". . . Be fruitful and multiply, and fill the waters in the seas, and let birds multiply on the earth" (Genesis 1:22).* Just think how many animals it takes to *fill* the seas—an immeasurable amount. Then God created mankind and says to them, *". . . multiply; fill the earth and subdue it . . ." (Genesis 1:28).* God wants the earth *filled* with animals and with people.

We can only estimate the population of the earth. New estimations say there are about 330 million people in the United States and over 7.7 billion in the world. Even so, God wants people to be so numerous they fill the earth, and only He knows when the earth reaches that number.

A BIG God

To speak of quantity, we can look at the universe with all of its stars—so many stars experts are not sure if even the estimates are close to being accurate. As for the estimate of stars in our galaxy (the Milky Way) astronomers give estimates ranging from 200–400 billion. If the estimates vary for stars in the Milky Way that much, how can an accurate estimate of stars in the universe be made? An accurate estimate seems impossible since it is estimated there are hundreds of billions of galaxies in the universe. It is safe to say that the actual number of stars is far beyond our comprehension.

Even though we are only seeing the smallest fraction of the stars (about two-thousand five hundred stars with the naked eye at any one time) it is hard to look into the sky at night and think God does not love quantity. When King David looked at the number of stars—which are simply the work of God's *fingers*—He declared:

> *When I look at the night sky and see the work of your fingers—the moon and the stars you set in place—what are people that you should think about them, mere mortals that you should care for them? (Psalm 8:3–4 NLT)*

The created universe is enormous. Even so, the third heaven (God's realm) is even larger than the created universe. God is BIG! God is *so big* that He fills heaven and earth.

> *"No one can hide so that I can't see him,"* declares the LORD. *"I fill heaven and*

earth!" declares the LORD. *(Jeremiah 23:24 GW)*

God's BIG Love

Earth, with all of humanity, is the smallest of specks in God's creation; yet, He infinitely cares for us. As *big* as God is, that is how *big* His love is. He has enough love to love each one of us infinitely.

Although heaven was filled with numerous created creatures experiencing the love of God, He still wanted more beings to share His love with—so He created humans in His image and even became a man and died for us so we can be with Him forever!

Even that kind of love for you was not enough—the Father wanted more than you just being with Him forever—He wanted you to be a *bride* for His Son!—to be *one* with His Son (see Ephesians 5:31–32). And to be one with Himself (see John 17:20–23).

Is it possible to understand such love in this lifetime? Yes, to a degree it is.

And may you have the power to understand, as all God's people should, how wide, how long, how high, and how deep his love is. May you experience the love of Christ, though it is too great to understand fully. Then you will be made complete with all the fullness of life and power that comes from God. (Ephesians 3:18–19 NLT)

Meditate on the above prayer for God is able to do more than you can ask or think. Go ahead; ask God for the things in the above Scripture since He wants you to understand the love He has for you.

God's love is not understood with the head, but with the heart. The only way to truly understand His love is to experience it—to have a relationship with Him. This requires spending personal time with Him in prayer and contemplation of His love for you.

God's BIG Harvest

Jesus tells us the harvest is abundant in Luke 10:2, ***"The harvest truly is great."*** When God says something is "great"—meaning abundant or plentiful—then it is huge. Yes, the end-time harvest is huge!

> ***When he looked out over the crowds, his heart broke. So confused and aimless they were, like sheep with no shepherd. "What a huge harvest!" he said to his disciples. (Matthew 9:36–37 TMSG)***

Jesus is still moved with compassion today as He sees an even greater multitude needing a shepherd. No doubt He is saying to us today, "What a *huge* harvest!"

Think about this, "If the harvest was huge in Jesus' time when there were relatively few people living on earth, what is it now with over 7.7 billion people alive?" To say the least, it is massive! Therefore, I have no problem believing a billion people will be born again in a short time—in one great wave. We are now in the beginning stages of the greatest harvest ever—a multitude no one can count.

After these things I looked, and behold, a great multitude which no one could number, of all nations, tribes, peoples, and tongues, standing before the throne and before the Lamb . . . (Revelation 7:9)

When the harvest is *for God Himself,* do you think it will be small? No! The end of the age produces the end-time harvest from every tribe, tongue, and nation and it is massive!

Having said all this, what will be the nature of the end-time harvest? It will be *both* quality and quantity—a harvest of a great multitude who are disciplined followers of Christ.

In the next chapter, we will discuss a "problem" with the harvest.

Chapter 5

The Problem

The harvest is not automatic; other things must take place before the harvest can come. Without these other things, there will not be a harvest. This is what I am calling "the problem."

God's Provision

God desires the end-time harvest and is birthing that desire in His people. More than ever, there is a cry for harvest resonating in His disciples, which is the first step in birthing it.

If the desire for the harvest is being birthed in His people, what else needs to happen? Two additional things must take place before there will be a harvest. No one explains this better than Jesus does in Matthew 9:36–38:

> *But when He saw the multitudes, He was moved with compassion for them, because they were weary and scattered, like sheep having no shepherd. Then He said to His disciples, "The harvest truly is plentiful, but the laborers are few. Therefore pray the Lord of the harvest to send out laborers into His harvest."*

We should notice three things in this passage:

1. It is *His* harvest. God is the Lord of the harvest; He will provide everything necessary for His harvest.

The first thing necessary is to feel His heart for His harvest—His compassion for people.

2. The *prayer* to the Lord of the Harvest is not a general prayer, but a specific prayer—to send out laborers into His harvest.

3. It takes harvest *laborers*, and not just a few.

Compassion, prayer, and labor are the prerequisites for the great end-time harvest. The Holy Spirit initiates these three things, but we must respond to His promptings.

Harvest Laborers

God's heart for His harvest, and the things necessary for it, stand out beautifully in Romans 10:13–15:

> *For "Everyone who calls on the name of the Lord will be saved." But how can they call on him to save them unless they believe in him? And how can they believe in him if they have never heard about him? And how can they hear about him unless someone tells them? And how will anyone go and tell them without being sent? That is why the Scriptures say, "How beautiful are the feet of messengers who bring good news!" (NLT)*

These verses brilliantly describe the harvest laborers. God sends laborers into His harvest with the good news so people can trust in Jesus, call upon Him, and be saved.

The Dilemma

We have a dilemma and a solution. The dilemma is God sees an abundant harvest but few laborers to harvest them. The solution is for God to work through men and women as they pray for workers. This includes being willing to be the answer to the prayer—to be laborers in His harvest.

God relies on the compassion, prayers, and labor of people to fix the problem of too few laborers. Does that mean God is placing faith in humans to get the job done? No, not actually. The Father's trust is in His Son's death, resurrection, and the power they released, which the Holy Spirit applies to our lives. God's confidence is in His workmanship He created through Christ by His Spirit. He believes in the work of His Spirit and the price His Son paid for the harvest.

For we are His workmanship, created in Christ Jesus for good works, which God prepared beforehand that we should walk in them. (Ephesians 2:10)

God Is for Us

God gives us everything we need to live a life pleasing to Him and to put our talents to use in His harvest. If God is for us, then who are we to resist His work in us? He is only trying to make us like His Son so He can say to us, *"Well done, good and faithful servant."*

We are predestined to be like His Son—to have His heart for the harvest and to lay down our lives for it.

For whom He foreknew, He also predestined to be conformed to the image of His Son, that He might be the firstborn among many brethren. . . .

What then shall we say to these things? If God is for us, who can be against us? He who did not spare His own Son, but delivered Him up for us all, how shall He not with Him also freely give us all things? (Romans 8:29–32)

This is the process we are in now—God conforming us into His Son's image for the sake of the harvest—*"that He might be the firstborn among many brethren."* Notice God says "many brethren," showing us again that the harvest is large. With this verse, He also connects the great harvest with His children being Christlike—*"conformed to the image of His Son."*

Use It or Lose It

If we do not use our talent, we will lose it according to Jesus' teaching in Matthew 25:28: *"Therefore [because he did not use his talent] take the talent from him, and give it to him who has ten talents".* The phrase "Use it or lose it" sounds harsh, but this is what Jesus said the kingdom is like. We have no justification for not using our talent; we only have excuses. Our excuses cannot stand before God's provisions for us. We have been given everything we need to fulfill our destinies:

His divine power has given us everything we need for life and godliness through our knowledge of him who called us by his own glory and goodness. Through these he has given us his very great and precious promises, so that through them you may participate in the divine nature and escape the corruption in the world caused by evil desires. (2 Peter 1:3–4 NIV)

We have a responsibility to use what God has provided for us. If we do, we can be conformed to the image of His Son. 2 Corinthians 7:1 makes our responsibility clear:

Because we have these promises, dear friends, let us cleanse ourselves from everything that can defile our body or spirit. And let us work toward complete holiness because we fear God. (NLT)

We are responsible for what God gives us and to do whatever He tells us to do. Stop sinning; for it hinders God's process of creating the image of His Son in us.

We have all the help we need to use our talents. We have the Holy Spirit as our helper to do what God calls us to do; we simply must do it.

Part One Conclusion

As you have noticed, this book is divided into three parts: THE HARVEST, THE PRAYER, and THE LABOR. THE HARVEST part of this book came first so we would know what we are praying and laboring for—the harvest.

In the next part of this book, we will discuss things you may not have thought of concerning prayer. These new perspectives of prayer will help you in the harvest.

Part Two:

THE
PRAYER

Chapter 6

What Is Prayer?

Before we begin this section on prayer, I want you to know more about myself. I have been praying for most of my life (I was born again over forty-four years ago). However, I still feel like a novice in prayer. Yes, I have spent countless hours in prayer and have seen many answers to prayer; nevertheless, I still consider prayer as one of my weak points.

Let me take a moment to share my experiences in prayer over the last forty-four years. I have gone for days without praying and I have gone for days not doing much besides praying. I have been in "dead" prayer meetings and in prayer meetings that "take your breath away." I have been the shy person praying in the corner of the prayer meeting and I have been the prayer leader. I have been the last person anyone would ask for prayer and I have been the Prayer Pastor of a church. I have gone from not being able to pray at dinnertime to spending all night in prayer many times. Currently, the vast majority of my prayer time is spent praying in the Spirit—praying in tongues.

I consider myself a very experienced "novice" in prayer. In other words, I am not an expert on prayer, just experienced in prayer. Therefore, I can relate to many people's prayer experiences as I share my own observations about prayer.

The following chapters on prayer will challenge you as they have me. And hopefully, all of our prayers for the harvest will improve from the principles of prayer shared in these chapters.

Our Teacher

We need new understanding about prayer not just "new" teaching; that is, we need a new comprehension of what Jesus already taught about prayer. He is the most insightful teacher ever on prayer.

The disciple who expects new understanding about prayer will ask Jesus to teach him or her about prayer. The disciples in the first century did just that, they asked Jesus to teach them to pray. If the disciples who walked with Jesus needed taught how to pray, we are no exception; we also need Jesus to teach us how to pray.

Those early disciples waited with anticipation as Jesus began to teach on prayer:

> *. . . one of His disciples said to Him, "Lord, teach us to pray . . ."*
> *So He said to them, "When you pray, say:*
>
> *Our Father in heaven,*
> *Hallowed be Your name.*
> *Your kingdom come.*
> *Your will be done*
> *On earth as it is in heaven.*
> *Give us day by day our daily bread.*
> *And forgive us our sins,*
> *For we also forgive everyone who is*
>   *indebted to us.*
> *And do not lead us into temptation,*
> *But deliver us from the evil one."*
>   *(Luke 11:1–4)*

Jesus continued His teaching on prayer a few verses later:

> *"So if you sinful people know how to give good gifts to your children, how much more will your heavenly Father give the Holy Spirit to those who ask him." (Luke 11:13 NLT)*

Jesus concludes His teachings on prayer in Luke 11 by saying that the Father will give the Holy Spirit to those who ask. Ask for the Holy Spirit because He is our Helper, our Teacher, and He will give us new understanding about prayer; He will bring all things Jesus taught to our remembrance.

> *"But the Helper, the Holy Spirit, whom the Father will send in My name, He will teach you all things, and bring to your remembrance all things that I said to you." (John 14:26)*

We need the Holy Spirit to remind us of what Jesus taught concerning prayer, which is the most profound teachings. The following is a quote from a previous book I wrote:

> *Jesus made prayer simple, not complex. By doing this, Jesus showed us prayer is not some religious exercise but is simply talking to our Father in heaven. That is, prayer is not for show, but for connection and relationship with God the Father. Still, your Heavenly Father wants you to ask Him for the things you need; however,*

*because He already knows your needs, you can
keep your requests simple and to the point.*
—Steven J. Campbell
The Christian's Bill of Rights, pg. 47.

The profound is in the simple because the simple is the most profound. Maybe that is why Jesus said, ***"Out of the mouth of babes and nursing infants You have perfected praise" (Matthew 21:16).*** Don't think children can't pray; their prayers may be the most profound.

Prayer

Prayer can be defined, but is best experienced. Prayer is not simply an exercise in words or thoughts; it is an experience unique to each individual. Definitions have their place, but an experience is greater than a definition. Nevertheless, the following is one of my definitions of prayer: *Prayer is simple; it is an experience with God.*

Prayer seems best when it is like a phone conversation between two people deeply in love—sometimes you are listening and sometimes you are talking. At other times, neither is saying anything; you're just enjoying having the other's attention. This type of conversation may go on for several minutes. In addition, with a relationship like this, your prayer may just be a simple "call" to say, "I love you" and then you "hang-up."

For those that have not prayed before, or not very often, prayer is like a telephone conversation between those just getting to know one another. At this stage, the first conversation is the hardest—to get the courage to call. On the other hand, a person may be hesitant to call not knowing what to say, or thinking they need the perfect words.

When we first begin to pray, we may not realize God has been waiting for our "call," and that He was not as concerned about what we say as much as the fact we finally prayed. Why? Because He loves us and wants us to start "calling" and building our relationship.

> *Call to me and I will answer you. I'll tell you marvelous and wondrous things that you could never figure out on your own. (Jeremiah 33:3 TMSG)*

Here is one more of my definitions of prayer: *Prayer is communication with God based upon our relationship.* Granted, you could add many things to this definition; however, this definition takes prayer from something explained to something experienced.

Prayer is not based upon words or thoughts, but upon relationship. Out of your relationship with God come the thoughts and words in prayer. Because of this, prayer is experienced differently for every individual. And even that individual will experience prayer differently as their relationship with God increases. To say all of this in different words, *your relationship with God determines what prayer means to you.*

Prayer is not static. Prayer is experienced differently every day because His mercies are new every morning (Lamentations 3:22–23). Plus, how you experience prayer is affected by the mood you are in that day.

If you want to know what prayer is, you will have to pray—to have a relationship with Father, Son, and Holy

Spirit. But be warned, it is like other relationships; if you want a close and rewarding relationship with God, you will have to be open and vulnerable. If you just want religious sounding prayer that does not open your heart to God, then you will have an unsatisfying, distant relationship. To get the love relationship with God your soul desires, you will need to be open and honest in prayer—not religious.

Just as we need the Bible to teach us about any relationship, we need taught about our "prayer relationship." Only One understands prayer perfectly—the man Christ Jesus. Therefore, He is the only perfect teacher about prayer relationship.

Let's look at the "Lord's Prayer" again and expound upon it further. This time we will quote from Matthew 6:9–13:

> *In this manner, therefore, pray:*
> *Our Father in heaven,*
> *Hallowed be Your name.*
> *Your kingdom come.*
> *Your will be done*
> *On earth as it is in heaven.*
> *Give us this day our daily bread.*
> *And forgive us our debts,*
> *As we forgive our debtors.*
> *And do not lead us into temptation,*
> *But deliver us from the evil one.*
> *For Yours is the kingdom and the power*
> *and the glory forever. Amen.*

Jesus FIRST showed prayer as a relationship—**"Our Father in heaven."** His teaching on prayer compares our relationship with His relationship to the Father in heaven. No doubt, Jesus wanted His disciples to know they too had a relationship with the Father and that is where prayer starts—"*Our* Father."

Jesus also used the term "Our Father" because He is your father only as Jesus is your savior. In other words, **if** Jesus is your Lord, then Jesus' Father is your Father also. Therefore, you can pray "Our Father" because you have relationship with Jesus. Whenever we pray "Our Father," or even just "Father," we should remember the significance of those words—we have relationship with the Father in heaven only because we first have relationship with Jesus Christ.

Additionally, we see that Jesus keeps this model prayer in the plural with the words "us" and "our." He does this because we are not an island to ourselves—we are members of one another. We are to bear one another's burdens as well as to take responsibility for ourselves.

> *If someone falls into sin, forgivingly restore him, saving your critical comments for yourself. You might be needing forgiveness before the day's out. Stoop down and reach out to those who are oppressed. Share their burdens, and so complete Christ's law. If you think you are too good for that, you are badly deceived.*
>
> *... Don't be impressed with yourself. Don't compare yourself with others. Each of you must take responsibility for doing the creative best you can with your own life. (Galatians 6:1–5 TMSG)*

Jesus taught us to pray to the Father in heaven. He personalized our prayers—pray to "Our Father." Fathers are not supposed to be far off, or someone we do not know. However, a sad fact is too many today do not know their earthly fathers.

We do not know what happened to Jesus' earthly father, Joseph, for it appears he died sometime between when Jesus was 12 and 30 years old. We know he was alive when Jesus was about 12 but apparently dead before Jesus started His ministry at about 30. Therefore, Jesus can identify with those whose father died while young or those not having an earthly father.

When Jesus shows us we can have a relationship with the Father in heaven, He is speaking about a personal father-child relationship with God. This father-child relationship is exactly what we are created for and desire most. This is available to "whosoever will" by simply believing in the Lord Jesus Christ.

For Lovers

Again, what is prayer? Prayer is for lovers. Prayer is to make you a lover of God by receiving the love He has for you. Prayer is for relationship, for fellowship, and for communion (common union). The "Mary-Martha story" shows us there are differences in experiencing the love of God. Mary and Martha both loved Jesus, but had different degrees of intimacy (see Luke 10:38–42).

We can have all of the relationship with God we desire. We can have the "Song-of-Solomon-type relationship" if we desire it. The Song of Solomon is written for that purpose—to be an example of the relationship to God we

WHAT IS PRAYER? 61

can have, showing the possibilities of our love for one another.

As we all know, marriages show different degrees of intimacy—some are close and some are not. A marriage relationship is based upon the principle of sowing and reaping—you get out of it what you put into it. The principle of sowing and reaping applies to prayer also, for the more we sow into prayer, the more we will reap from it.

I have found that prayer is like my marriage relationship—sometimes I am upset with my wife and do not want to talk or listen to her. Likewise, at times I have been upset with God and did not want to talk to or listen to Him. Even so, like in my marriage, I come "to my senses" and realize our relationship is more important than my hurt feelings; then it is back to relationship, companionship.

Every Part of Us

What is prayer? Prayer includes your mind, body, soul, and spirit.

1. Prayer may come from the *mind*—you finally figure out, "God, I need Your help!"

2. Our *body* language may also be a prayer—lifting your hands in surrender.

3. The *soul* may be emotional as you cry out to God in prayer.

4. The *spirit* of man is where we have the deepest relationship with God because God is Spirit (see John 4:23–24).

Right Motives

Prayer helps you make right choices for the right reasons. When you fellowship with God you begin to see things as He does—your perspectives change. Love becomes a central motivation for your actions. You make choices based upon, "What would love (Jesus) do?" Then as you pray, Jesus is able to impart His heart about the situation.

If Jesus thought it necessary to pray before making important decisions, we must too. He spent all night in prayer before He chose the twelve apostles because He had to make the right choices for the right reasons.

> *Now it came to pass in those days that He went out to the mountain to pray, and continued all night in prayer to God. And when it was day, He called His disciples to Himself; and from them He chose twelve whom He also named apostles. (Luke 6:12–13)*

A Warning

Jesus wants prayer to be about relationship with the Father, so He gives us stern warnings in Matthew 6:5–9:

> *And when you come before God, don't turn that into a theatrical production either. All these people making a regular show out of their prayers, hoping for stardom! Do you think God sits in a box seat?*

Here's what I want you to do: Find a quiet, secluded place so you won't be tempted to role-play before God. Just be there as simply and honestly as you can manage. The focus will shift from you to God, and you will begin to sense his grace.

The world is full of so-called prayer warriors who are prayer-ignorant. They're full of formulas and programs and advice, peddling techniques for getting what you want from God. Don't fall for that nonsense. This is your Father you are dealing with, and he knows better than you what you need. With a God like this loving you, you can pray very simply. . . . (TMSG)

God's Idea

Prayer is God's idea; it is His idea for building relationship with us. Prayer is a wonderful gift from God for knowing Him and is man's highest calling—to experience God in His fullness (see Ephesians 3:19). We can know God through prayer!

For the Harvest

This book is discussing prayer as it relates to the harvest. Prayer for the harvest becomes easier when you are praying for others to experience relationship with your Father in heaven. Why? Because once you experience the love of the Father, you want others to also. Then, you will pray for the Father to send laborers into His harvest and you will want to be one of those laborers.

Chapter 7

God Is Approachable

One of the foremost teaching moments for all of us is in the third chapter of Genesis—a lesson we must all learn. What is the lesson? The lesson is that God is love. When we truly know this, it will show in our response to Him when we sin—we will respond differently.

Adam and Eve

From Adam and Eve's response to God, it is obvious they had a great deal to learn about God's love. The Scripture says they hid themselves from the *presence* of the LORD. Why? Because they had disobeyed Him and were afraid of being confronted by Him since they now knew they were naked—they became self-aware—"took their first selfie."

We know the devil was there and active in helping them to sin. I wonder if he was also speaking lies to them after they sinned, such as: "God is going to get even with you for this;" or "God does not want anything to do with you now;" or "You should be ashamed of yourself."

Obviously, they were not thinking: "I hear God walking in the garden; He is coming to help me;" or "I need to run to God for help;" or "God loves me so much He will forgive me and help me out of this."

God was not shocked or surprised when Adam and Eve sinned. He knew the exact moment they sinned against Him; yet, He came as usual to meet with them. God even called out to Adam, "Where are you?" which was not just a question to gain information about his whereabouts. It was the cry of God's heart. Because man was made for fellowship, God's heart was crying out for it. Yes, His heart was *grieved* over their sin, but because He is pure love, He was wanting to restore their relationship.

The Lesson

Without question, it is mankind who breaks fellowship with God and becomes afraid of Him because of their sinful condition. Even so, from the beginning, God teaches us *He* makes a way for us to approach Him and to fellowship with Him. He makes the way by providing a covering for our nakedness (our sinful condition). Unfortunately, we often try to cover ourselves, and as Adam and Eve discovered, our coverings for sin do not make God approachable.

Adam and Eve hid from God because they knew their "fig-leaf-clothes" did not cover their sin. They needed God to make them a covering (Genesis 3:21). Only one covering for sin makes God approachable—the blood of Jesus.

You may ask, "What about all of the Old Testament sacrifices for sin?" All the Old Testament sacrifices were only an effective covering for sin because they foreshadowed Jesus' blood sacrifice, which validated all these sacrifices. The Old Testament sacrifices pointed *ahead* to Jesus' sacrifice just as our partaking of communion points *back* to Jesus' sacrifice. The communion of the bread and cup is valid only because of Jesus' death on the cross. Your covering for sin is the *person* who sacrificed Himself—Jesus. He is your covering for every sin you ever committed—things you should have done but did not do, and the things you did do.

The main lesson to learn is God wants *your* fellowship. He wants you to run to Him if you sin, not hide from Him. For God is available to help you when you need Him the most. *"God is our refuge and strength, an ever-present help in times of trouble" (Psalm 46:1 GW).*

The Obstacle

We discussed in the last chapter that prayer is about relationship. But how can we have a good relationship with someone we are not sure wants a relationship with us? That is a good question, and this chapter is for dealing with that major obstacle to prayer.

How do we know God wants a relationship with us? Because the moment He gave His Son for us, He rent the veil of the temple from top to bottom. Why did He do that? Because the veil of the temple hid Him from everyone except the High Priest—who could only enter His presence once a year. But when Jesus died on the cross, God tore the veil so He could get out of that place of limited fellowship. God is out in the open now and everyone can come to Him through Christ.

The beginning and the end of the Bible show God calling people to come to Him.

The Spirit and the bride say, "Come!" And let him who hears say, "Come!" Whoever is thirsty, let him come; and whoever wishes, let him take the free gift of the water of life. (Revelation 22:17 NIV)

What is a major obstacle to prayer? It is when you are not sure if God is approachable. You may think that "the minister" can freely approach God, but you are not sure if you have the same freedom. At times, you may have thought everyone else has more freedom to God's presence than you do. The truth is that *you* can have boldness in approaching God through His covering for your sins.

God's Eternal Purpose

Through Jesus Christ and His blood sacrifice, you can confidently approach God. Ephesians 3:11–12 declares:

> *This was his eternal plan, which he carried out through Christ Jesus our Lord.*
>
> *Because of Christ and our faith in him, we can now come boldly and confidently into God's presence. (NLT)*

God's eternal plan has always been to enable access to Him *only* through Jesus Christ. Jesus is called the ***"lamb slaughtered before the creation of the world" (Revelation 13:8 GW).*** We also see this truth in other Scriptures.

> *Long before he laid down earth's foundations, he had us in mind, had settled on us as the focus of his love, to be made whole and holy by his love. Long, long ago he decided to adopt us into his family through Jesus Christ. (What*

pleasure he took in planning this!) (Ephesians 1:4–5 TMSG)

God Wants You

God wants you! He always has wanted you; He gave His only son for you. You see, God desired fellowship with you before the earth existed—long before you were born. God has always desired for you to be able to approach Him through His Son Jesus Christ, and in approaching Him, to experience His great love for you. It grieves Him when you think He does not want your fellowship. He is hurt when you ignore Him, or do not turn to Him in time of need first. If you are a parent, you can understand this because of your relationship with your children. All your children may be in fellowship with you, but if one of them ignores you, it hurts. So it is with God—your relationship to Him matters regardless of how many others are in fellowship with Him.

Let's put all this in the context of prayer. In times of prayer, you have the honor of expressing your love to Him and receiving His love for you. Certainly, the more you understand His desire for you, the easier it is to break through the flesh and all the spiritual warfare and pray to your heavenly Father.

Are You Worthy?

As we discussed in the beginning of this chapter, when Adam and Eve sinned God came as usual to meet with them calling out to Adam, "Where are you?" For the first time He had to call out to them because they were hiding from Him since they felt unworthy. They had sinned and did not believe God was approachable now. Even so, God made the first move—He initiated the fellowship after they sinned because He wanted to cover their sin and shame.

God wants to cover all our sin and shame too; we simply must come to Him if we sin. Let's be bold in faith and come before Him for His cleansing. Let's decide to break the cycle of hiding from God's presence when we feel unworthy. The truth is God wants us moving toward Him when we feel the most unworthy for this shows our faith in His love for us.

Do you think Moses felt worthy of God's presence when he had murdered a man? Did David feel worthy after he committed adultery and murdered the husband to cover it up? Yet, these men freely enjoyed going boldly into God's presence, receiving His forgiveness.

Do not believe the devil's lies. He will tell you that you are unworthy since you sinned. He will even remind you of certain Scriptures to make you feel unworthy (of course, he leaves out the part about what Jesus has done for you). Your worthiness is not from yourself; it is from Christ. The Father has assigned Jesus' righteousness to you; therefore, in Christ, you are worthy. Our faith in Jesus is our righteousness.

> *But if you see that the job is too big for you, that it's something only God can do, and you trust him to do it—you could never do it for yourself no matter how hard and long you worked—well, that trusting-him-to-do-it is what gets you set right with God, by God. Sheer gift. (Romans 4:5 TMSG)*

If you do sin, your responsibility is to repent (be sorry for your sin, ask for forgiveness and change your way of living). Do not make excuses for your sin. Tell God exactly what you did with as little pretense as possible. Remember, God knows all of the sordid details and He wants you to ask Him to forgive you without excuses. God forgives sin, not excuses, as John declares in 1 John 1:9–10:

> *If we confess our sins, He is faithful and just to forgive us our sins and to cleanse us from all unrighteousness. If we say that we have not sinned, we make Him a liar, and His word is not in us.*

Don't let feelings of unworthiness keep you from praying. In Jesus, we can come boldly before God and obtain mercy and grace in our time of need (see Hebrews 4:14–16). So when you feel unworthy, pray!

Praise

Praise should be a major part of our prayers. We approach God with praise because He made us worthy to stand before Him; His love ripped the "curtain" for us to enter into fellowship with Him. Jesus' body was the "curtain" torn for us to enter boldly into God's presence.

> *And so, dear brothers and sisters, we can boldly enter heaven's Most Holy Place because of the blood of Jesus. By his death, Jesus opened a new and life-giving way through the curtain into the Most Holy Place. (Hebrews 10:19–20 NLT)*

Praising God is often thought of as just singing songs of praise. Yet, praise is more to than that. For example, when we think of praising something or someone, we do not think of singing a song. Praise is an attitude of the heart that comes out of the mouth.

> *. . . For out of the abundance of the heart*
> *the mouth speaks. (Matthew 12:34)*

To be emotional in prayer is acceptable to God since He gives you your emotions for intimate fellowship with Him (and with others). When your heart is filled with thankfulness and praise to God, it flows from your mouth in your prayers.

In John chapter 17, Jesus was very emotional in prayer—with thanksgiving and praise. And in Luke 22:39–46, Jesus was so emotional in prayer that His sweat became like blood. Because of Jesus' example, you do not have to be afraid of being emotional in prayer since you are fellowshipping with an emotional God! He loves your emotions because they are a vehicle for intimacy with Him. He relates to your emotions as no one else can, which creates a special intimate relationship. When your prayer time includes praise and thanksgiving, it creates a most intimate fellowship with your Father.

> *Enter into His gates with thanksgiving,*
> *And into His courts with praise.*
> *Be thankful to Him, and bless His name.*
> *(Psalm 100:4)*

Entering God's presence with thankful prayers causes peace to flood our hearts. Philippians 4:6–7 tells us to:

Never worry about anything, but in every situation let your requests be made known to God in prayers and petitions, with thanksgiving. Then God's peace, which goes far beyond anything we can imagine, will guard your hearts and minds in Christ Jesus. (ISV)

Sealed by God

When Jesus sent the promise of the Father (the Holy Spirit) to us, it sealed the fact that God is approachable. How? Because He approached us first, giving us His Spirit.

... And when you believed in Christ, he identified you as his own by giving you the Holy Spirit, whom he promised long ago. The Spirit is God's guarantee that he will give us the inheritance he promised and that he has purchased us to be his own people. He did this so we would praise and glorify him. (Ephesians 1:13– 14 NLT)

To sum up what we have said: In Christ, God is approachable; we can approach Him through prayer in whatever condition or emotional state we find ourselves.

In the next chapter, we will answer the question, "Is it hard to pray?"

Chapter 8

Is Praying Hard?

Human beings do not like to fail; in fact, fear of failure keeps many from fulfilling their destiny. As you may recall from the first chapter of this book, one of the servants did not use his talent because of fear. His fear took on two basic forms: 1) A fear about his relationship with his master; 2) A fear of losing the talent (fear of failure). Because of these fears, he hid his talent resulting in a severe rebuke from his master—*"You wicked and lazy servant."*

The kingdom of heaven is like the *Parable of the Talents*—some hear praise and some hear rebuke depending upon how their talents are used. The purpose of this book is to help us hear, *"Well done, good and faithful servant."*

In the last chapter, we covered the first form of fear, fear concerning our relationship with the Master. In this chapter, we will cover the fear of failure as it relates to prayer.

The Issues

People neglect prayer when they don't think they'll be successful in prayer. I want to restate this more personally: I have neglected prayer at times because I did not believe prayer would really help. Now, let me personalize it for you: You have neglected prayer when you did not think it would help, or at least not very much.

Given that prayer is a major lifeline in our relationship with God, we do not want anything hindering it. The first step in avoiding hindrances to prayer is knowing what the obstacles are. This chapter will help us understand the obstacles and challenges of prayer, answering the question, "What makes prayer harder than it should be?"

Answering this question may help us overcome the fear of failure in prayer. However, we will have to be honest enough to look deep within ourselves to see why we have not prayed more often.

Here are three hindrances making prayer harder than it should be: 1) Not knowing God's will; 2) Little faith in God; 3) Personal warfare. We will look at each hindrance individually.

1) Not Knowing God's Will
When we are in doubt about God's will, we will not be sure of our success in prayer. To be successful in prayer, we must be confident in God and know His will.

> *Now this is the confidence that we have in Him, that if we ask anything according to His will, He hears us. And if we know that He hears us, whatever we ask, we know that we have the petitions that we have asked of Him. (1 John 5:14–15)*

There are three major ways to discern the will of God. We will look at this key first—the Bible.

A) THE BIBLE
The Bible is the foundation for knowing the will of God; by knowing what it teaches, we can know His

will for much of our life. That does not mean a person could not know the will of God if they do not have a Bible. Even so, those believers not having a Bible pray for one, since the Scriptures reveal God's will for them. They often have a greater hunger for the Scriptures than most with Bibles.

God has blessed this generation with more Bibles and Biblical teaching than any other generation; yet, many seem to struggle to know the will of God not taking advantage of all God has given them. Far too many of us have multiple Bibles unread. We have received these "talents of gold" and instead of using them, we have hidden them under the cares of this world. We shouldn't let the cares of this world smother the Word of God so that it becomes unfruitful in our lives.

Knowing the will of God allows us to have confidence in our prayers—we know we will be successful. Additionally, by knowing the Scriptures we can examine what others teach—like the people in Acts 17:11, *". . . every day they carefully examined the Scriptures to see if what Paul said was true" (GW).*

B) THE HOLY SPIRIT

Another major way to know the will of God is by the Holy Spirit. The Father sent the Holy Spirit to live within us to know His will. Jesus said the Holy Spirit would be our teacher and help us remember what He taught (see John 14:26).

If we follow the leading of Holy Spirit, we will be doing the will of God. Also, Holy Spirit helps us to pray according to the will of God even when we do not know His will.

Now He who searches the hearts knows what the mind of the Spirit is, because He makes intercession for the saints according to the will of God. (Romans 8:27)

When we pray by the Holy Spirit, we always pray according to the will of God and we can expect total success in those prayers.

C) KNOWING GOD

Another major way to know the will of God is by knowing Jesus *personally.* Jesus said His sheep know His voice. This is an intimate knowledge of His voice, which results in knowing His will. To know God personally through the Bible, the Holy Spirit, and His presence, is the best way to know His will and to have confidence in your prayers.

2) Little Faith in God

The second hindrance making prayer harder than it should be is deficient faith in God. Jesus emphasized faith in God and praying in faith saying, *"Have faith in God. . . . whatever you ask for in prayer, believe that you have received it, and it will be yours" (Mark 11:22–24 NIV).*

Many do not find success in prayer because they do not pray in faith. The Scriptures inform us that if we do not pray in faith, we will not receive anything from the Lord:

> *. . . ask in faith, with no doubting, for he who doubts is like a wave of the sea driven and tossed by the wind. For let not that man suppose that he will receive anything from the Lord . . . (James 1:6–7)*

Faith is essential in prayer. Even so, to be successful in prayer we may have to cry out to Jesus like the man did in Mark 9:

> *Jesus said to him, "If you can believe, all things are possible to him who believes." Immediately the father of the child cried out and said with tears, "Lord, I believe; help my unbelief!" (Mark 9:23–24)*

Unbelief is a major hindrance to prayer. In addition, many "worry-pray" (to pray because they are worried) not realizing Jesus calls this "little faith." Worriers are not confident God will take care of them (see Matthew 6:25–34). We need to recognize worry as a hindrance to successful prayer.

We should ask Jesus to root out all unbelief and worry from of our hearts; for we do not want to hear Him say to us, *"O you of little faith" (Matthew 6:30)*. We want Him to say to us what He said to the centurion who only needed Jesus to speak the word—He said he had "great faith" (see Matthew 8:10). To be successful in prayer, we need to believe God.

3) Personal Warfare
The third major hindrance that makes prayer harder than it should be is personal warfare. Let's start with this question, "Is prayer easy, or is it hard?" Your answer to

this question can influence your prayer life. In your mind, you may have answered this question already; if you did, you probably answered it based upon your experience in prayer. The following thoughts in this chapter are designed to challenge your ideas about personal warfare in prayer. When you think praying is a struggle, you will answer the question above as, "Prayer is hard!" But is that the case? Might it be you are struggling against something besides prayer? Yes, for the struggle is not with prayer, the struggle is with the flesh!

A) THE FLESH

Jesus clearly identifies the struggle when His disciples could not pray with Him for one hour.

> *Then He came to the disciples and found them sleeping, and said to Peter, "What? Could you not watch with Me one hour? Watch and pray, lest you enter into temptation. The spirit indeed is willing, but the flesh is weak."*
> *(Matthew 26:40–41)*

Jesus expected His disciples to pray with Him for one hour because their spirit was willing to pray; however, the disciples allowed their flesh to rule over their spirit. The struggle is with the flesh. When you allow flesh to rule over your spirit, your flesh will be empowered; then you can easily enter into any temptation. In the example above, instead of praying the disciples gave into the flesh and slept, ignoring Jesus' warning to them—*"Watch and pray, lest you enter into temptation."* These disciples would not have entered into temptation, if they had yielded to their spirit and prayed.

What does "the flesh is weak" mean? It means the needs of your physical body may easily override your spiritual needs since physical needs seem more urgent than spiritual needs. Many times prayer is delayed until later because it seems less urgent than your physical needs.

"The flesh is weak" does not mean it does not have strong desires. Actually, the phrase means the flesh is *too* strong and is ruling over your spirit.

Your "flesh" includes your will and your emotions. Your will and emotions (your feelings) are the hardest things to submit to the Lord and must be ruled over.

Jesus wrestled with His "flesh-will" in the Garden of Gethsemane. His flesh (body, will, and emotions) was like ours and He had to overcome it. In fact, He was resisting His flesh so hard that an angel came from heaven to strengthen Him; and as He continued to battle in prayer, His sweat became like drops of blood.

Jesus wrestled *in* prayer not *with* prayer. He was wrestling with His flesh, not with prayer. Luke 22:42–44 declares:

> *Father, if it is Your will, take this cup away from Me; nevertheless not My will, but Yours, be done.*
>
> *Then an angel appeared to Him from heaven, strengthening Him.*

And being in agony, He prayed more earnestly. Then His sweat became like great drops of blood falling down to the ground.

Let's get this out of the way—praying can be hard because your flesh is weak. But Jesus said to take up your cross daily. Why? Because it is a fact that we know all too well, flesh does not want to die—it wants to have its way. But those who are Christ's have crucified the flesh with its passions and desires. Galatians 5:16–17, 24 says:

I say then; Walk in the Spirit, and you shall not fulfill the lust of the flesh.

For the flesh lusts against the Spirit, and the Spirit against the flesh; and these are contrary to one another, so that you do not do the things that you wish.

And those who are Christ's have crucified the flesh with its passions and desires.

Praying may seem hard because we must overcome our weak flesh. Essentially, our greatest warfare in prayer is our weak flesh.

B) THE SPIRITUAL RULERS

Another aspect of our personal warfare is the spiritual warfare outside of us.

> *For we do not wrestle against flesh and blood, but against principalities, against powers, against the rulers of the darkness of this age, against spiritual hosts of wickedness in the heavenly places. (Ephesians 6:12)*

Although some write on this subject extensively, we will not, except to say, *"Do not fear, for those who are with us are more than those who are with them" (2 Kings 6:16)*.

This subject is worth far more chapters than what I can give it in this book. Even Jesus needed to spend time dealing with the devil and his powers; so we are not saying it is unimportant; it is just not the purpose of this book to cover it in detail.

C) THE SPIRIT

The best part of personal warfare is our spirit being willing to pray and war. Our spirit is not afraid of the warfare, whether from without or from within.

The Holy Spirit makes praying easy because it **flows** out of the heart. Apparently, about 500 were called to wait in the upper room for the baptism of the Holy Spirit, but only 120 made it to Pentecost—not because prayer is hard, but because the flesh is weak. Even so, those 120 who were baptized in the Holy Spirit found out how easy prayer can be. Praying is easier than many realize!

Prayer is easy when you pray in the Spirit. You may groan and travail in the Spirit, but even that is "easy" compared to "praying in the flesh."

Jesus would spend all night in prayer. Have you ever tried that? I have prayed all night many times and it was hard because of the weakness of my flesh. However, because my spirit was willing, I prayed. Staying awake and keeping the desire to pray was hard because my flesh wanted to sleep; however, my spirit loved it—that is why I did it for one day a week for years.

Praying is not hard; because the spirit is willing. Taking time to pray can be hard because the flesh is weak and wants its way, which can be challenging to overcome.

Jesus knows all about our weaknesses—He was tempted with His flesh as we are, but He overcame. And through His victory over the flesh, we too can have the victory in Christ—overcoming our flesh.

Don't focus on prayer as hard but as "easy" because the spirit is greater than the flesh. Don't let the flesh rule over your spirit. The flesh and everything concerning the flesh will die, but your spirit will live forever.

Jesus said the Holy Spirit will flow out of us as rivers of living water:

> *"He who believes in Me, as the Scripture has said, out of his heart will flow rivers of living water." But this He spoke concerning the Spirit, whom those believing in Him would receive . . . (John 7:38–39)*

It does not sound hard to pray in the Spirit since the rivers of living water *flow* out of us by the Holy Spirit. We are emphasizing this because what we think about prayer will determine how, when, or if we pray.

Now, back to *The Parable of the Talents*, the "wicked and lazy servant" did not use his talent because he thought it was just too hard and he would fail. When you are afraid of failure in prayer because it is just "too hard," you will not pray—at least not much. Then, when you fail to pray, you are planning to fail.

Use your talent—Pray! It is the best investment you can make.

Chapter 9

Why Pray When God Knows?

People often think of prayer as simply asking for things from God. With that in mind, an obvious question arises because of what Jesus said in Matthew 6:8, *"... For your Father knows the things you have need of before you ask Him."* The question is: "If the Father knows what we need *before* we ask Him, why does He want us to ask?" The answer to this question is multi-faceted.

First, asking God for something acknowledges our need for Him. When we ask for God's assistance, it shows we are not relying upon our own strength, but upon His strength.

Second, asking God for what we need confirms the vital relationship that we have with Him—the Father-child relationship. A child naturally asks his father for the things he has need of, even if the father already knows their need. Jesus spoke about this in Matthew 7:7–11 when He said:

> *Ask, and God will give to you. ... Yes, everyone who asks will receive.... If your children ask for bread, which of you would give them a stone? Or if your children ask for a fish, would you give them a snake? Even though you are bad, you know how to give good gifts to your*

children. How much more your heavenly Father will give good things to those who ask him! (NCV)

Jesus speaks of the obvious things here, "bread and fish," because all children need to eat and their fathers know that. Of course, children will still ask for their physical needs even if their fathers know their needs. Without question, it is the nature of a child-father relationship for the child to ask the father for their needs.

Third, Jesus established the model of asking for our needs (daily bread) when He said to pray in this manner:

> *In this manner, therefore, pray:*
> *Our Father in heaven,*
> *Hallowed be Your name.*
> *Your kingdom come.*
> *Your will be done*
> *On earth as it is in heaven.*
> *Give us this day our daily bread.*
> *(Matthew 6:9–11)*

Fourth, God has given us the responsibility for the earth; therefore, He usually does not do things upon the earth unless we ask Him to. Psalm 115:16 states, *"The heaven of heavens is for GOD, but he put us in charge of the earth"* (TMSG).

Since we have been put in charge of the earth, God waits for a prayer from us to do what needs to be done. God knows what we need but usually waits for us to ask Him for what is needed.

David marveled at how God created the heavens with His fingers, setting the moon and stars in their place, yet the

Lord looked to man to rule over the works of His hands. Psalm 8:3–6 declares:

> *When I consider your heavens, the work of your fingers, the moon and the stars, which you have set in place, what is man that you are mindful of him . . . ?*
>
> *You made him ruler over the works of your hands; you put everything under his feet. (NIV)*

The Lord expects us to rule over the earth, but not without His help. He wants us to ask Him for whatever we need to rule in our realm of life.

Fifth, in the last several decades, America has been asking God to leave many areas of society resulting in man trying to cope without God's help. Consequently, America has been on the decline. Even so, America is now waking up and asking God for help in every area of society. It starts with Christians asking God for what they need so they can be the light of the world. We are a light when we set the example of asking God for everything we need.

Sixth, even though we have asked God for something, He encourages us to keep on asking—be persistent in prayer.

> *So I say to you: Keep asking, and it will be given you. Keep searching, and you will find. Keep knocking, and the door will be opened for you. For everyone who keeps asking will receive, and the person who keeps searching will find, and the person*

who keeps knocking will have the door opened. (Luke 11:9–13 ISV)

Jesus instructs us to be persistent in prayer, even when God already knows what we need. Nevertheless, He does warn us about using vain repetition. *"And when you pray, do not use vain repetitions . . ." (Matthew 6:7).* Vain repetitions are not the same as persistent prayer. Vain repetition is trying to impress God, yourself, or others with your prayer by praying the same thing over and over to make it last longer and be more impressive. Vain repetition is for impressing someone (sometimes you are even trying to impress yourself). Vain repetition comes from the mind; persistent prayer comes from the heart. Also, you may have noticed that when you pray in the Spirit there is usually repetition.

Prayer is more than just "saying a prayer." Too many just "say a prayer" instead of praying. Praying involves experiencing relationship, not just saying words. We have all "prayed" at times without really praying. Praying involves actually speaking to God and not just saying words off the top of our head.

Seventh, God wants us to pray even though He knows what we are going to pray because He wants our fellowship—the communication with us. Prayer is for relationship and not just getting our needs met. When we "say a prayer," we are not experiencing the fellowship God desires. He wants us to pray to Him so we can experience Him. At times, the greatest prayer can be one simple word, JESUS!

Prayer is for enjoying the Lord! Enjoying the Lord is not difficult because He is the most enjoyable person imaginable; so much so, we will enjoy Him forever!

A final reason to pray when God already knows our need is that He delights in answering our prayers. It pleases Him to give us the things of His kingdom. Jesus said it this way:

> **Do not fear, little flock, for it is your Father's good pleasure to give you the kingdom. (Luke 12:32)**

It gives The Father great joy to answer your prayers. And the joy of the Lord is your strength, which has a two-fold application. First, you can have a measure of His joy when you see the answer to your prayer. That is, as His child, you feel His joy in giving you the answer. Second, when you see the joy He has in answering your prayers, that is your strength; because it's not just about answering your prayer; it is about you. He has such joy over you! He likes you! His joy is about you, not just answering your prayer. To know His joy over you gives you strength. If He is for you, who can be against you? Now that is true strength.

Chapter 10

Is it All About God?

Is it all about God? This is a great question since we hear this statement often, "It's all about You, Lord." Is there anything wrong with this statement? The answer may surprise you. The answer is two-fold—"Yes" and "No." Scripture shows the two sides to this issue. In one respect, it is all about God; in another respect, it is not all about God. Now, we will give the Scriptures to support what we are saying.

All About God

According to Colossians 1:18, it is all about the Lord:

> *And he is the head of the body, the church; he is the beginning and the firstborn from among the dead, so that in everything he might have the supremacy. (NIV)*

Then in 1 Corinthians 15:28, we see, without a doubt, *it is all about God!*

> *Now when all things are made subject to Him, then the Son Himself will also be subject to Him who put all things under Him, that God may be all in all.*

God's Heart

Still, there is an aspect where it is not all about God. This aspect is found *in the heart of God.* You see, God is love and is not all absorbed in Himself. He says that love, ***"... doesn't think about itself" (1 Corinthians 13:5 GW).*** From God's side, it is not just all about Him; it is also about what He loves. We see this in John 3:16, ***"For God so loved the world that he gave his one and only Son . . ." (NIV).***

Some may still think John 3:16 is all about God. However, according to God's definition of love, love is not self-seeking. Love is not about self; it is about another. John 3:16 does not say, "For God so loves Himself." His love is about us—that is why He gave His Son.

When you love someone, is it just all about you and the love you have? Or, is it just about the other person? Or, is it about both of you? Love is not an island to itself. Love is meant to be shared—that is why God has so many in heaven and on earth to share His love with.

Father God

When you get to know this wonderful God called Father, you realize His heart is that of a father—He wants children with Jesus being the firstborn. Jesus, who knows the Father's heart better than anyone else, left the Father and came to earth so He could give the Father children through His sacrificial life and death on the cross—now we are called the children of God!

To sum up what we are saying so far; from our side, it is all about God; from God's side, it is not all about Him. We see this in one of God's greatest acts in the Old Testament when He brought the children of Israel out of Egypt with many mighty signs and wonders. Indeed, from our perspective, it was all about God. Nevertheless,

God had a shockingly different perspective when speaking to Moses about it in Exodus 32. God said it was *Moses* that brought his (Moses') people out of Egypt. ***"And the LORD said to Moses, 'Go, get down! For your people whom you brought out of the land of Egypt . . ." (verse 7).*** Then in verse 11, Moses said God brought them out of Egypt:

> ***Then Moses pleaded with the LORD his God, and said: "LORD, why does Your wrath burn hot against Your people whom You have brought out of the land of Egypt with great power and with a mighty hand?"***

Moses saw it as all about God; God saw it as Moses being an integral part of His work. Why are we saying all of this? Does it really matter? Yes! Because when we understand this, it affects our prayers. We will have more faith that our prayers make a difference in our circumstances, or even in the state of affairs in nations!

Moses seemed to have some understanding of this when his intercession saved the Israelites from the destruction God had planned. Moses interceded, having God remember His promises. Moses prayed in Exodus 32:13, ***"Remember Abraham, Isaac, and Israel, Your servants, to whom You swore by Your own self . . . So the LORD relented from the harm which He said He would do to His people"*** ***(Exodus 32:14).*** Wow! By understanding God's love is not self-seeking (all absorbed in Himself), we can remind Him in prayer about His faithful servants and it moves His heart. This is an amazing passage of

Scripture, for we see it is not just about what God wants apart from how it affects humanity. Exodus 32:10 is also a shocking verse because we see God asking a man to let Him do what He feels like doing. Verse 10 says, *"Now therefore, let Me alone, that My wrath may burn hot against them and I may consume them. . . ."*

2 Chronicles 7:14

This principle applies to one of the most used verses in these times, 2 Chronicles 7:14.

> *Then the LORD appeared to Solomon by night, and said to him: "I have heard your prayer, and have chosen this place for Myself as a house of sacrifice. When I shut up heaven and there is no rain, or command the locusts to devour the land, or send pestilence among My people, if My people who are called by My name will humble themselves, and pray and seek My face, and turn from their wicked ways, then I will hear from heaven, and will forgive their sin and heal their land. Now My eyes will be open and My ears attentive to prayer made in this place." (2 Chronicles 7:12–15)*

God hears the prayers made in His house. We are the house of God since His Spirit dwells in us, and God is attentive to our prayers. Understanding these principles will help to deliver us from a fatalistic view of God— "What will be, will be." For God wants us to know our teaching, preaching, praying, etc., make a difference in His dealings with the world.

Jonah

In Jonah 3:1–10, we see the same pattern as in 2 Chronicles 7:13–14. The pattern is: 1) God's judgment is revealed, 2) Men humble themselves, praying, seeking God, and turning from their wicked ways, 3) God relents from the judgment.

Jonah's repentance and obedience resulted in the salvation of Nineveh. Even so, we need to be delivered from any trace of Jonah's wrong attitude concerning God's loving kindness to others:

> *Jonah was furious. He lost his temper. He yelled at GOD, "GOD! I knew it—when I was back home, I knew this was going to happen! That's why I ran off to Tarshish! I knew you were sheer grace and mercy, not easily angered, rich in love, and ready at the drop of a hat to turn your plans of punishment into a program of forgiveness!*
>
> *"So, GOD, if you won't kill them, kill me! I'm better off dead!" (Jonah 4:1–3 TMSG)*

More Examples

First, Jesus said it is all about God when asked about the greatest commandment—love God with everything you have and everything you are. Then, Jesus kept on speaking and let us know that there is something more— *"And the second is like it: 'You shall love your neighbor as yourself'"* *(Matthew 22:39).* It is all about loving God, but there is still something more—love others also.

The second example is when Jesus asked Peter if he loved him—it was not just all about Him; it was also about Jesus' people. He told Peter that if he loved Him, he had to take care of His sheep (see John 21:15–17).

The third example is when you actually encounter God; at that time, you will experience both man's perspective and God's perspective. In Isaiah chapter 6, Isaiah encounters God and is undone; he knew like never before that it is all about God. Then we come to verses 8 and 9 where the heart of God is revealed:

> *Also I heard the voice of the Lord saying:*
>
> *"Whom shall I send,*
> *and who will go for Us?"*
>
> *Then I said, "Here am I! Send me."*
> *And He said, "Go, and tell this people . . ."*

The fourth example is when Jesus prays in John 17. He prays about Himself and His Father, as well as spending a large portion of His prayer for us.

The fifth example is found in John 3:16 and Isaiah 53 both showing us it is about God *and* us. Jesus gave His life for the Father, and He laid down His life for the sheep—two sides of the same story.

The sixth example is how God is not our servant; He is to be served, right? Yes, from our side, but Jesus said He did not come to be served, but to serve—He made Himself a servant (see Matthew 20:28). We serve God, but He serves us. He serves us in the Holy Spirit, our Helper, and with His angels.

Until you know it is all about God, you will not understand His heart. Amazingly, it is the Father's dream to be on the earth with His people. For when it is all about God, it includes us!

Even when it is about us humans, it is still about God. Galatians 4:19 says, *"I am in labor until Christ is formed in you."* When it is about us, it is about *Christ* being formed in us.

A House of Prayer

By understanding God's commitment to us in answering our prayers, it helps us to be faithful with our prayer "talent." We realize the importance of prayers for the harvest and will ask for laborers helping to fulfill the Scripture: *"My house shall be called a house of prayer for all nations" (see Isaiah 56:7).*

Chapter 11

Praying in Truth

If Jesus were to speak to the church today, what would He say? The answer is profound but simple: He would speak out of His nature—He is full of grace and full of truth (see John 1:14). Therefore, whatever He would speak to the church would be truth and grace.

Because He is the same yesterday, today, and forever (Hebrews 13:8), we have a Scriptural basis to know what He would say—He would speak as He has spoken in the past.

The Revelation of How Jesus Speaks

How did He speak to the churches in the past? We see the answer in Revelation chapters two and three. These two chapters reveal the heart of Jesus as He speaks to *His* church—He speaks to her with fullness of grace and truth. In these chapters, Jesus speaks to the seven churches of the first century. Many believe these seven churches in Asia also represent seven eras of church history with the Laodicean church being the church at the end of the age. Even so, we do not want to overlook Jesus' messages to all of the churches since He has a message for every type of church. He has a message for any church which:

1) Left its first love.

2) Is persecuted or poor.

3) Is a compromising and worldly.

4) Is immoral.

5) Is lifeless.

6) Is faithful.

7) Is lukewarm.

I believe the church that most represents our day is the Laodicean church, the lukewarm church. Why would Jesus call the church of our day lukewarm?

> *"Because you say, 'I am rich, have become wealthy, and have need of nothing'—and do not know that you are wretched, miserable, poor, blind, and naked . . ."* *(Revelation 3:17)*

Jesus speaks the truth to us without compromise because lukewarmness blinds our eyes to our current condition; and unless He tells us the truth by His grace, we will never change. Therefore, He reveals our true condition so we can change course.

How to Change Course

So how can we change? Jesus tells us:

> *I counsel you to buy from Me gold refined in the fire, that you may be rich; and white garments, that you may be clothed, that the shame of your nakedness may not be revealed; and anoint your eyes with eye salve, that you may see. (Revelation 3:18)*

Lukewarmness is hard to overcome since we think we are fine; we feel we have everything we need. In fact, we do not know how poor we are until Jesus speaks the truth to us; then, when we know the truth, we can be set free. Jesus speaks the truth to us in love: *"As many as I love, I rebuke and chasten. Therefore be zealous and repent" (Revelation 3:19).*

Jesus is standing at the door of His church knocking to see if anyone is hearing what He is saying—if anyone will open his or her heart inviting "The Truth" (Jesus) to come in. For those who do, He promises a place of ultimate authority. *"To him who overcomes I will grant to sit with Me on My throne, as I also overcame and sat down with My Father on His throne" (Revelation 3:21).*

A throne speaks of authority. The end-time church is promised ultimate authority if she will overcome her lukewarmness by opening her heart to The Truth. He wants us to have authority to overcome the ultimate darkness at the end of the age, but it will not be given to the lukewarm; it will be given to those who overcome lukewarmness.

Pray Truthfully

Applying what we are speaking of to prayer, you need to pray in truth. If you are lukewarm, acknowledge it before God and ask Him for the "gold refined in the fire and the white garments." And if you think you are not lukewarm, ask God to show you your true condition, it may surprise you.

We are emphasizing what Jesus spoke to the lukewarm church, but all of Revelation chapters two and three may apply to us. Personally, I have also been deeply challenged by what Jesus spoke to the church in Revelation 2:4–5:

> *. . . you have left your first love.*
>
> *Remember therefore from where you have fallen; repent and do the first works, or else I will come to you quickly and remove your lampstand from its place—unless you repent.*

These words hit me hard because I remember my first love, and to some degree, I have left my first love. Jesus' grace is when He confronts me with this truth. His grace is the truth spoken to me. When I receive the truth spoken to me, then I can pray truthfully:

> *"God, I have left my first love in some ways and I want it all back! Help me Jesus by Your Holy Spirit to see how far I have fallen from my first love. Unless you show me where I have fallen from my first love, I will think I am still in a good place when I am not. Speak the truth to me by your Spirit so I know what to repent from, and then help me to repent. I ask for all of this through Jesus, Amen."*

True Grace

Extreme teachings about grace are going around now; they are not the truth. Grace does not allow you to do whatever you choose. Grace enables you to walk in the truth. Grace does not freely allow sin in a Christian's life. The Scriptures address this issue in Romans 6:1–2 declaring, *"What shall we say then? Shall we continue in sin that grace may abound? Certainly not! How shall we who died to sin live any longer in it?"*

Do not believe anyone who says it is okay to sin because we are living under grace (sin is doing what God says we should not do). It is never acceptable to sin when we are under grace:

> *What then? Shall we sin because we are not under the law but under grace? Certainly not!*
>
> *Do you not know that to whom you present yourselves slaves to obey, you are that one's slaves whom you obey, whether of sin leading to death, or of obedience leading to righteousness? (Romans 6:15–16)*

James Chapter Four

James chapter four is full of grace and truth, but it is hard to read since it confronts us head-on. Verse one says, *"Where do wars and fights come from among you? Do they not come from your desires for pleasure . . .?"* Then verse 3 says, *"You ask and do not receive, because you ask amiss, that you may spend it on your pleasures."*

Here are a few examples of not praying in truth:

1) Praying for a material blessing so others will see how God has blessed you because you are so "spiritual."

2) Praying for a person's healing hoping they are healed so you will get the recognition (glory).

3) Praying and hoping God will punish the person you "forgave" for their sin against you.

Praying truthfully is praying in line with the teachings of Scripture. If we are not careful, we will find ourselves praying in line with our pleasures instead of what is in line with the Word of God. The extreme teachings on grace lead to fulfilling our pleasures more than fulfilling the Word of God. True grace is not about fulfilling our pleasures but about fulfilling *His* pleasure.

The Way and the Warning

Jesus is the way to God—the only way. He is the grace of God revealed. If you want to know true grace, you must know Jesus Christ. When He gives us a warning, it is His grace speaking. His warnings are true because He is truth. Do not let any person deceive you that they know the way when they contradict The Way—Jesus Christ.

Jesus is not after your pleasure; He is after you pleasing the Father. If you please the Father, it will be your ultimate pleasure. Without a doubt, standing before Him and hearing the words, "Well done, good and faithful servant" will cause you to "enter into the *joy* of your Lord." And there is no greater joy than entering God's joy.

Jesus' warnings are for making sure you please the Father and enter into His joy. One of Jesus' most sobering warnings is found in Matthew 7:21–23:

"Not everyone who says to Me, 'Lord, Lord,' shall enter the kingdom of heaven, but he who does the will of My Father in heaven. Many will say to Me in that day, 'Lord, Lord, have we not prophesied in Your name, cast out demons in Your name, and done many wonders in Your name?' And then I will declare to them, 'I never knew you; depart from Me, you who practice lawlessness!'"

We are living in the days of lawlessness increasing and Jesus warns us of this lawlessness and its consequences. He warns us that **most** will grow cold because of lawlessness and that we are not going to make it unless we endure to the end:

"And because there will be more and more lawlessness, <u>most</u> people's love will grow cold. But the person who endures to the end will be saved" (Matthew 24:12–13 GW, emphasis added).

His grace lets us know that certain practices will keep us out of the kingdom of God. Galatians 5:19–21 declares:

When you follow the desires of your sinful nature, the results are very clear: sexual immorality, impurity, lustful pleasures, idolatry, sorcery, hostility, quarreling, jealousy, outbursts of anger, selfish ambition, dissension, division, envy, drunkenness, wild parties, and other sins like these. Let me tell you again, as I have before, that anyone living that sort of life will not inherit the Kingdom of God. (NLT)

Truth is grace, and grace is truth. Grace speaks the truth or it is not grace speaking. The truth is Jesus and His Word—the Scriptures.

Created Equal

All men and women are created equal in the sense that *every* life is valuable to God. He is not willing that any should perish but that all should come to the knowledge of the truth—to come to Jesus (see 2 Peter 3:9 and 1 Timothy 2:4).

Not all are equal in the sense of their birth in worldly status. Some are born into poverty, some are born neither poor nor rich, and some into great wealth. The *Parable of the Talents* that we started this book with shows how some are given more riches (talents) than others are. Even so, each person has the same opportunity to use what they have even though their "talents" are different. The main thing is that we *use* our giftings. Romans 12:6 states, **"Having then gifts differing according to the grace that is given to us, let us use them . . ."**

We are all equal in the sense of having a life to glorify God with by using what we have, whether great or small. However, Jesus says that it is hard for a rich person to enter into the kingdom of heaven (see Matthew 19:23). Does that mean we should not want to be rich? It depends upon our motive. Is it just for looking good before others as "a person blessed of God?" Or, is it for building up the Kingdom of God? Watch out, this can be a tricky one because we can easily justify the motives of our heart. We will need to examine our heart's motive frequently because our motive may easily be to establish our own personal ambition or agenda. These are the days when God will be transferring great wealth to people for the massive harvest (people who will use it for His glory).

For the eyes of the Lord run to and fro throughout the whole earth, to show Himself strong on behalf of those whose heart is loyal to Him. (2 Chronicles 16:9)

Praying in Wisdom

Wisdom is a gift from God. It is knowing you need wisdom and praying for it. James 1:5 declares, *"If any of you lacks wisdom, let him ask of God, who gives to all liberally and without reproach, and it will be given to him."*

We all need the wisdom found in the Bible; the book of Proverbs is a great place to start—it personalizes wisdom and shows its beauty.

If God does not open our understanding of the Scriptures, we will be like Peter and the other disciples who tried to keep Jesus from suffering and dying. They did not have the wisdom of God in the situation because they did not understand what God was about to do. Wisdom always builds upon Christ, especially upon the cross. Wisdom understands His love—the laying down of His life. It understands that there is no greater love than laying down your life for another.

Peter proclaimed he would not deny Jesus like everyone else even though Jesus said he would. This was not wisdom; it was self-promotion. Jesus said to Peter, ***"Will you lay down your life for My sake? Most assuredly, I say to you, the rooster shall not crow till you have denied Me three times" (John 13:38).***

Jesus always went by the Scriptures, not by what His flesh would desire. He prayed in wisdom (He prayed Peter's faith would not fail; He did not pray he would not deny Him—see Zechariah 13:7; Matthew 26:31).

Paul prayed three times for a weakness to be taken away. Nevertheless, Jesus had the wisdom to allow Paul's weakness since His strength is made perfect in weakness. Therefore, it is wisdom to pray about our weakness to gain the Lord's perspective of it. Weaknesses that serve Him should stay; those that don't serve Him should go (see 2 Corinthians 12:7–10).

The kingdom of God is advancing rapidly in our time and the Scriptures tell us how we enter into it. ***"We must go through many hardships to enter the kingdom of God" (Acts 14:22 NIV).*** With this in mind, I ask, "Are our prayers hindering us from entering the kingdom?" Are we praying like Peter, "May it not be so Lord"? Or, do we have the wisdom to pray like Jesus did—that our faith will not fail? These are the days to know the truth that through **many** hardships we enter the kingdom. By accepting this truth, we can pray with greater wisdom.

Wisdom is to pray as David prayed in Psalm 139:23–24. He prayed for God to search him, to try him, and to lead him.

Jesus said the end-times would be like in the days of Noah. Consequently, we need to build an "ark" for the harvest. The "ark" we can build is our prayers for the harvest that are based upon the Word of God. When we pray for God to send laborers into His harvest, wisdom understands we will be one of the laborers.

Chapter 12

Healing and Communion

Our health is vital at the end of the age since God has much for us to do in His harvest and we need to be healthy enough to fulfill it. This includes all of the body of Christ as each member has a function in the harvest. Those handicapped physically or mentally are no exception; God has work for them too.

In the last few years, I have been challenged physically; I became handicapped, not able to do much of anything for myself. I was not able to attend church services for several months. Later, I was able to attend by using a wheelchair. The issue was not my handicap, but whether I was healthy enough to fulfill God's will for my life. The answer was, "No." As with myself, the issue is not whether you are handicapped or not, but whether you are able to do what God wants you to do.

The rest of my story is that the body of Christ rallied around me and God heard their prayers and delivered me from most of the handicap. I am now free to run and dance! Again, the issue is not whether you are handicapped in some way; the issue is whether you are healthy enough to accomplish God's will. You may need to pray about your current health situation to know what God would have you do about it. Many have found better health simply by changing their eating habits. Now, we come to an important question many ask, which I will attempt to answer.

Why God?

Often a question is the first step to the answer—if you want the answer, you need the question. However, we do not always receive *correct* answers to our questions. Correct answers belong to God and come from Him. With questions continuing to increase, the value of the Bible is increasing year by year, not decreasing as some are trying to proclaim. In fact, God's answers in the Bible will be sought out more and more at the end of this age.

In the Bible we find answers to our questions about health and long life, which enable us to fulfill our place in the harvest. We should not be too sick or too weak to do what God has called us to do, living long enough to finish our purpose on earth.

Many weak Christians ask God, "Why am I so weak?" Many sick Christians ask God, "Why am I sick?" Their friends also ask God the same questions. Then when someone's death seems premature, the most common question from everyone is, "Why God?"

Since these are such important and common questions, you would think God would have answered them in the Bible—and He did, at least to some extent. Yes, God does give us some clear answers; however, I do not believe He gives us *all* the answers at this time.

Before we explore one answer God gives us, we will look first at the word "many." Examples of words that mean the same or about the same as "many" are: numerous, countless, scores of, and several. When the Scripture uses the word "many" what does that mean? First, it does not mean "all." Second, it does mean "many." This especially applies to the Scripture we are about to quote.

In other words, this verse will not apply to *every* case of weakness, sickness, and death; but it does apply to *many* of the cases. With this in mind, let us look at an answer God gives us to the "Why?" question. The Biblical answer is:

> *For if you eat the bread or drink the cup without honoring the body of Christ, you are eating and drinking God's judgment upon yourself. That is why many of you are weak and sick and some have even died. (1 Corinthians 11:29–30 NLT).*

Many Christians are weak, sick, and a number die too early. Why? When partaking of the bread and cup, they do not honor Christ's body. What does that mean? It means we need to understand what we are doing when we partake of the communion.

Understanding the Communion

Understanding the communion is not difficult; we simply need to know and understand a few Scriptures. Even understanding the word "communion" may help us. This word is a joining of two words: "common" and "union." In partaking of the bread and the cup, we need to understand our common-union with Christ's body.

Jesus instituted the communion of the bread and cup as the Scripture states:

> *For I received from the Lord that which I also delivered to you: that the Lord Jesus on the same night in which He was betrayed took bread; and when He had*

given thanks, He broke it and said, "Take, eat; this is My body which is broken for you; do this in remembrance of Me." In the same manner He also took the cup after supper, saying, "This cup is the new covenant in My blood. This do, as often as you drink it, in remembrance of Me." (1 Corinthians 11:23–25)

We will look at three things to be understood about the communion. They are: 1) It represents our union with Jesus; 2) Jesus died for our healing; 3) We are all a part of the body of Christ. We will look at each of these points individually.

1) Our Union with Christ

The first thing to understand about discerning the Lord's body is to recognize what the bread and drink represent. Jesus is the bread and His blood is the drink that is symbolized in the bread and cup we partake of. Jesus proclaimed:

I am the bread of life. . . . I am the living bread that came down from heaven. If anyone eats this bread, he will live forever. And the bread I will give for the life of the world is my flesh."

. . . Truly, truly I tell you, unless you eat the flesh of the Son of Man and drink his blood, you do not have life in yourselves. The one who eats my flesh and drinks my blood has eternal life, and I will raise him to life on the last day. For my flesh is real

food, and my blood is real drink. The person who eats my flesh and drinks my blood remains in me, and I in him. Just as the living Father sent me and I live because of the Father, so the one who feeds on me will also live because of me. (John 6:48–57 ISV)

When we partake of the bread and cup, it represents us partaking of Jesus. It "re-presents" [to present again] what He did for us on the cross. Heaven's bread, Jesus, and His blood is what gives us eternal life. When we partake of the communion, we are signifying that we have common-union with Christ. If we do not have common-union with Christ but partake anyway, we partake in an unworthy manner. This is serious because God says:

For he who eats and drinks in an unworthy manner eats and drinks judgment to himself, not discerning the Lord's body. For this reason many are weak and sick among you, and many sleep (1 Corinthians 11:29–30).

Thank God for Jesus' death (the bread from heaven) that opens up our understanding of the Word of God. Only in Christ are the Old and New Testaments fully understood—His life and sacrifice give the full meaning to the Scriptures. The two disciples on the road to Emmaus experienced this.

While he was at the table with them, he took bread and blessed it. He broke the bread and gave it to them. Then their eyes were opened, and they recognized him. . . . They said to each other, "Weren't we excited when he talked with us on the road and opened up the meaning of the Scriptures for us?"

. . . Then the two disciples told what had happened on the road and how they had recognized Jesus when he broke the bread. (Luke 24:30–35 GW)

Jesus' death opened up the Scriptures (the Bible) for us. In Jesus, we can understand the Scriptures—including the communion. Indeed, spiritual revelation often comes to us while we partake of the bread and cup. If we are not partaking of Him (Jesus) by reading the Bible or by listening to the voice of the Holy Spirit, then that could be another answer to our "Why God" question—we may be weak or sick because we did not have our "daily bread." This is an important part of discerning the Lord's body—He is our Bread (our life). We need to partake of Him daily to be healthy.

2) Jesus Died for Our Healing

The Lord's body is given for our healing. His flesh was torn and broken so we can be healed. 1 Peter 2:24 states, **"He himself bore our sins in his body on the tree . . . By his wounds you have been healed" (ISV).** Peter knew this because of the Old Testament prophecy that Isaiah spoke of Jesus saying:

But he was pierced for our transgressions, he was crushed for our iniquities; the punishment that brought us peace was upon him, and by his wounds we are healed. (Isaiah 53:5 NIV)

Jesus' suffering and death provide spiritual and physical healing for us. He gave His flesh and His blood for us—when His flesh was torn and broken, blood poured out. The Bible tells us that the life is in the blood. Jesus' spilled blood is life for our physical bodies. His spilled blood and broken flesh are His provision for our healing.

To discern the Lord's body as provision for our healing is important. Our partaking of the communion represents our receiving what Jesus did for us—paying the price for our healing. We may be weak or sick because we did not understand this.

3) We Are Part of the Body of Christ

We need to discern the Lord's body as the "body of Christ." The context of the communion verses in 1 Corinthians 11 is that of the body of Christ—*the church.* When the Corinthian church met together, they were not honoring one another; they were being selfish, not waiting on others or considering the needs of others—even eating and drinking more than their share.

Jesus died for each one of us equally; therefore, we should honor one another—if we dishonor our church family, we dishonor Christ. When we do not think we need the other members of the body, we dishonor Christ. Might it be that "many are weak and sick and a number have died" because we have dishonored Christ by our unloving, unforgiving, unthankful, independent attitudes toward His body, the church? Is this what the Scriptures are saying? I think it is a major answer to the "Why God" questions.

We all need to be a part of a local church (the body of Christ). To think and act otherwise is to dishonor Christ and His body. If we discern the Lord's body correctly, we will be a part of it. If we are not a part of a local body of Christ, then we do not have the strength or power from it—another reason why many are weak.

God designed us to receive strength from the fellowship and prayers of the body of Christ. We all need this life-giving sustenance from the church. When we are joined to the body of Christ, we experience the life from the body. Just as our physical body resists sickness and tries to heal itself, so it is with the body of Christ. Healing and strength are in the body of Christ. 1 Corinthians chapter 12 explains this in much more detail; I will quote just three of the verses here:

> *The way God designed our bodies is a model for understanding our lives together as a church: every part dependent on every other part, the parts we mention and the parts we don't . . . If one part hurts, every other part is involved in the hurt, and in the healing.*
>
> *You are Christ's body—that's who you are! . . . Only as you accept your part of that body does your "part" mean anything. (1 Corinthians 12:25–27 TMSG)*

Our attitude concerning the body of Christ (the church) is central in 1 Corinthians 11, which is the chapter that informs us of our responsibility to not partake of the communion in an unworthy manner. As we have discussed, the warning about partaking of the bread and cup in an unworthy manner is clear. The following is a quote from another translation of these verses.

> *Every time you eat this bread and drink from this cup, you tell about the Lord's death until he comes.*
>
> *Therefore, whoever eats the bread or drinks from the Lord's cup in an improper way will be held responsible for the Lord's body and blood. With this in mind, individuals must determine whether what they are doing is proper when they eat the bread and drink from the cup. Anyone who eats and drinks is eating and drinking a judgment against himself when he doesn't recognize the Lord's body.*
>
> *This is the reason why many of you are weak and sick and quite a number of you have died. If we were judging ourselves correctly, we would not be judged. (1 Corinthians 11:26–31 GW)*

God's Heart

Jesus instituted the communion to be a blessing for us; but He wants us to know how serious it is when we do. If we partake in an unworthy manner it brings judgment upon us. God's heart is for each one to judge themselves correctly—examine yourself truthfully. Ask yourself, "Are you honoring the body of Christ?" The things we discussed earlier may help you answer that question truthfully. If there is sin in your life, it does not mean you cannot partake. It means you need to repent (change your mind and heart) *before* you partake.

God wants you to partake of the bread and cup as a reminder of what Jesus did and does for you. ***But let a man examine himself, and so let him eat of the bread and drink of the cup (1 Corinthians 11:28).***

In Hebrew 12:5–6, we see God disciplines those He *loves*. Therefore, God's judgment in 1 Corinthians 11:30 is about His love—His love for His Son and His love for you.

We want to restate the importance of our having strength, health, and long life. We need to be as strong and healthy as possible, living as long as necessary to fulfill our place in the end-time harvest. Otherwise, how will Jesus be able to say to us, "Well done, good and faithful servant"?

The heavenly Father wants us to have an intense yearning for His desire to be established on the earth. His desire is for His Son to be honored. We honor His Son by believing in who He is—the bread from heaven. In addition, we honor His Son by believing in all He did for us (see Isaiah 53). Last, but not least, we honor the Father's Son by honoring all of His brethren.

Therefore, we should be able to "run" to take the communion knowing that it symbolizes the power of Jesus to heal us—mind, body, soul, and spirit.

Healing Prayers

One of the important things in the harvest will be the healing of the sick. When Jesus walked the earth, He healed the sick. He is still doing the same today through His people. He said, *"Heal the sick, cleanse the lepers, raise the dead, cast out demons. Freely you have received, freely give" (Matthew 10:8).* Then He said in Mark 16:15–20:

> *. . . Go into all the world and preach the gospel to every creature. . . . And these signs will follow those who believe: In My name they will cast out demons; they will speak with new tongues . . . they will lay hands on the sick, and they will recover. . . . And they went out and preached everywhere, the Lord working with them and confirming the word through the accompanying signs.*

Jesus sent the Holy Spirit to *help* us. The Holy Spirit is the "helper," not the "goer" or "doer." We are to go and do the works of Matthew 10 and Mark 16. We are to go, lay hands on, and pray; that is our job. Then God works *with* us confirming the *word* with signs following. He is not just performing haphazard signs; He is confirming the word preached. In other words, the signs are confirming what we have shared about Jesus. If we have shared that Jesus is our deliverer from demons (addiction) then the signs will be mostly deliverances. If we share how Jesus is our healer, then the signs will be mostly healings; and if the preaching is about Jesus as our joy, then signs of joy will follow, and so on.

Jesus did not say to pray for the sick in Matthew 10, but to heal the sick. And in Mark 16, He did not say believers would just pray for the sick, but that they would heal the sick. Why? Because we can in our own strength pray for the healing of the sick, but we cannot heal in our own strength. Healing puts the focus on Jesus because He is the one that heals. Anyone can pray, but it takes Jesus' power to heal. Now is the time for the church to go from praying for the sick to healing the sick!

Yes, we need to pray for the sick, but we need to stop thinking that that is all we need to do. Jesus expects us to heal the sick. The harvest will not be brought in by simply praying for the sick; the harvest will come when the church heals the sick.

Healing Services

The church needs a revolution in our healing services. I believe we have hindered God's healing power because we have fallen prey to what I call the "Acts 3 syndrome." What is this syndrome? It is the looking at the power of men instead of the power of Jesus. Acts 3:11–12 says:

> *Now as the lame man who was healed held on to Peter and John, all the people ran together to them . . . So when Peter saw it, he responded to the people: "Men of Israel, why do you marvel at this? Or why look so intently at us, as though by our own power or godliness we had made this man walk?"*

How many times have we fallen into thinking it is a person's godliness or power that can heal? Yes, there are gifts of the Spirit certain ones have for healing, but it is not from them, it is a gift of the Spirit. A new believer can have the gift as easily as a "mature person" can. Any brand-new believer can pray for healings because healing is in the name of Jesus.

This is one of the emphases of Mark 16—you preach the gospel and those who believe your message will heal the sick. It does not say it is after they are mature, but it is simply a sign that they are a true believer—any believer can heal the sick!

Jesus' holiness and piety are what heals the sick, not a person's power or godliness. Therefore, if you are a believer in Jesus, you can heal the sick.

Maybe we need to have healing services where the new believers pray, or where the children pray—to help get us free of the "Acts 3 mentality." Moreover, if someone is believing God for a healing, maybe we should have someone we don't think is so pious pray for them.

Some have taken this a step further with remarkable results. I have heard of recent testimonies of Christians asking unsaved friends and loved ones to pray for them. These "unholy" ones were so touched by this that they began to open their hearts to the love of Jesus. Why? Because these believers humbled themselves before their friends and family and this broke the "holier than you attitude" and their friend's hearts were open to the gospel. Certainly, holiness is important. Our holiness allows the Holy Spirit to flow more freely through us; whereas sin grieves the Holy Spirit and can hinder His healing flowing through us (see Isaiah 59:1–2). However, God resists any prideful attitude concerning our holiness and gives grace to those that humbly admit that healing is from the Holy Spirit.

The harvest requires healings—healings that point to Jesus and not to us. As I heard someone say years ago, "If you will take the blame for someone not being healed, then you will take the credit for someone being healed."

Chapter 13

Prophetic Prayer

Part of my destiny was revealed to me about 25 years ago and had every cell in my body responding with, "Yes!" What is that part of my destiny? It is to pray end-time prophetic prayers.

The following is my part of how I see prophetic prayer. Prophetic prayer may sound a bit mysterious, but I believe it is simply knowing what God wants to do at a specific time and declaring or praying for Him to do it. The only "mysterious" part about it is knowing what God wants to do.

We *all* see in part and prophecy in part as 1 Corinthians 13:9 states, ***"We know only a portion of the truth, and what we say about God is always incomplete"*** *(TMSG)*. Accordingly, what I write now is my limited part about prophetic prayer. You may have a much greater understanding about prophetic prayer than I do, but you still need all the other parts to have a complete picture. I need your part of the picture and you need my part, for God created us to need each other.

Declaring and Praying

The first step in prophetic prayer is to know what God wants to do. The Scriptures are the key to this knowledge, revealing the will of God with the Holy Spirit revealing the timing of a particular Scripture. We see an example of prophetic declaration in the life of Simeon. He knew the Scriptures prophesied about the birth of a savior; nevertheless, he did not know the timing of the Lord until the Holy Spirit revealed it to him.

> *. . . there was a man in Jerusalem whose name was Simeon . . . And it had been revealed to him by the Holy Spirit that he would not see death before he had seen the Lord's Christ.*
>
> *So he came by the Spirit into the temple. And when the parents brought in the Child Jesus . . . he took Him up in his arms and blessed God and said:*
>
> > *". . . my eyes have seen Your salvation Which You have prepared before the face of all peoples,*
> > *A light to bring revelation to the Gentiles,*
> > *And the glory of Your people Israel."*
> > *(Luke 2:25–32)*

Prophetic prayer is *to declare or to pray the current will of God into a situation.* Simeon's prophetic prayer was a *declaration* of the Scripture; he prophetically declared Jesus' destiny—God's salvation—even for the Gentiles.

An example of *praying* a prophetic prayer is in Daniel 9. Daniel knew from the Scriptures it was God's timing for Jerusalem, so he prayed for God to move on Jerusalem's behalf (see Daniel 9:2–3).

Nothing is more prophetic than the Scriptures. Plus, praying from the Scriptures assures us of the answer to our prayers since we know that we are praying according to God's will.

This is the confidence that we have in approaching God: that if we ask anything according to his will, he hears us. And if we know that he hears us—whatever we ask—we know that we have what we asked of him. (1 John 5:14-15 NIV)

Our Uniqueness

Jesus gives us a Scriptural way to pray; we call it "The Lord's Prayer." As we have previously discussed, this prayer is an *example* of how to pray. It is not to be memorized word for word and prayed the same for everyone.

God is creative; therefore, we are not all the same. We are all unique individuals; consequently, God wants prayer a million different ways. We see how God loves uniqueness in the four gospels—the same Gospel, but told in four unique ways. It is: The Gospel *According to* Matthew, The Gospel *According to* Mark, The Gospel *According to* Luke, and The Gospel *According to* John.

We all have a unique perspective on the good news, and God likes it that way. When we talk about the four gospels, it is a little confusing because there is only one gospel; nevertheless, that one gospel is to be shared in our own unique way. So it is with praying the "Lord's prayer." It is great to all pray it together in the same words at times, even though each one prays it with different understanding and depth. So in that respect, praying the same prayer is still praying it uniquely.

When God prophetically opens the Scriptures, each one receives the same message differently. Matthew, Mark, Luke, and John have one gospel expressed in four different ways because they are four unique individuals, which gives greater depth to the gospel. The same is true for us, we all have a part of the gospel to share and the more parts we put together, the more beautiful and fuller the gospel becomes.

My perspective of prophetic prayer is that it deals with the *current* will of God. To me, the "Lord's Prayer" is a prophetic prayer because it deals with God's current will. It has a unique application for each person praying it: 1) His will being done on earth as it is in heaven, 2) A person's daily bread, 3) The need of forgiveness and forgiving others, and 4) Issues of temptation.

Jesus said the gospel of the kingdom would be preached in all the world at the end of the age. Since we are living in the end-time, we can declare and pray for laborers to fulfill His word—to preach the gospel of the kingdom in all the world.

In these days, another excellent prophetic prayer to declare or pray is 2 Thessalonians 3:1–2, *". . . that the message of the Lord may spread rapidly and be honored . . . that we may be delivered from wicked and evil men . . ." (NIV).*

The cross is the basis for the power of prophetic prayer. Without the cross (His death, burial, and resurrection) there would be no gospel—no victory to declare or to pray for.

The prayer of Jesus in John 17 and the prayers of the Apostles in the Bible are always excellent for prophetic declarations and prayers. We also find that the Old Testament is filled with things to declare and pray.

Jesus said that we would do the works that He did and even greater works because He went back to His Father in heaven (see John 14:12). Jesus did the "work of prayer." Consequently, we too will pray as He did and even greater. How can we do that? For sure, I do not know how, except to say that it will be by the Holy Spirit praying through us.

We are to be baptized in the name of the Father, Son, and Holy Spirit—to be immersed into the Father, into the Son, and into the Holy Spirit. We are to have their concerns—He is concerned about the great harvest at the end of this age. The great harvest is all the people that are to be saved from every nation of the earth. These are the Father's children, the Son's bride, and the Holy Spirit's temple. The Father desires the Son's bride, the Son is yearning for the Father's children, and the Father and Son are longing for temples of the Holy Spirit.

At the end of the age, more and more people will experience prophetic prayer for the great end-time harvest.

Chapter 14

Praying in Unity

I s everything just about those who are alive at this present time; or, is it about what God did in the past, is doing in the present, and will do in the future? Too often we have acted as though it is all about us, forgetting about what God has already done through His people in every generation. Even so, those who are alive now are vitally connected to every previous generation.

Those alive at the end of this age will be only a part of what God is doing—an important part because they will sum up an era of history, but only as a part of history. History is "His-story" of things past, present, and future. God is called the One who is, who was, and is to come (see Revelation 11:17). All of history is summed up in Christ; this is why Jesus is called The First and The Last, The Beginning and The End, The Alpha and The Omega. Jesus is the central part of *all* of history—God's story.

Even though the end-time generation will fulfill an era of history, their lives will include what God has done in the past. Because of this, it is an insult to God to think He is doing something through us not related to what He already did. That is, His Kingdom is from everlasting to everlasting—it is not just about us who are still alive, but it is about all God does in every generation. For this reason, we need to be joined to what God did through others—even from the beginning of time. We see this in John 4:34–38:

> *Jesus told them, "My food is doing the will of the one who sent me and completing his work. . . . The one who harvests is already receiving his wages and gathering a crop for eternal life, so that the one who sows and the one who harvests may rejoice together. For in this respect the saying is true: 'One person sows, and another person harvests.' I have sent you to harvest what you have not labored for. Others have labored, and you have entered into their labor." (ISV)*

Jesus sent us to harvest by being joined with the labor of others throughout history. Because of this, we can pray into *all* of their labor—especially those who have labored in prayer, even if they died long ago. In that sense, all of us, alive and dead, have our prayers coming together at the end of the age for the great harvest. God will use the prayers from all generations to fulfill His purposes. These prayers will move the hand of God as He harvests the earth as we see in Revelation 5:8 and 8:1–6. The power of *all* the prayers of the saints throughout history releases the end-time works of God—the harvest of the good and the bad.

Our end-time prayers for the harvest are important to God, but they are not the only prayers He uses. He mixes our prayers with the prayers of all of the saints throughout history combining the "old" prayers with the "new" prayers.

The Old Testament ends with Malachi 4:6, which is no accident since verse 6 connects the Old and New Testaments. It speaks of the fathers being connected to the children and the children being connected to the fathers. This does not just speak of the biological fathers and biological children; it also speaks of the Jews (fathers) being connected to the Christians (children) at the end of the age. In other words, it is the Jews and Gentiles coming together. Malachi 4:5–6 states:

> *See, I will send you the prophet Elijah before that great and dreadful day of the LORD comes. He will turn the hearts of the fathers to their children, and the hearts of the children to their fathers; or else I will come and strike the land with a curse. (NIV)*

This does not just refer to parents and their children as many have limited it to; it also refers to the "one new man" spoken of by the Apostle Paul. What is the result of both the Jews and Gentiles coming to Christ? It is life from the dead—which includes the great harvest (see Romans 11:15).

Completing the Labor

The labor of the fathers is not complete without us. This does not speak of only the Old Testament saints; it also speaks of all the saints who have gone before us. They need us, and we need them, for God wants our faith and their faith to be joined as the Scripture states:

> *Not one of these people, even though their lives of faith were exemplary, got their hands on what was promised. God had a better plan for us: that their faith and our faith would come together to make one*

> *completed whole, their lives of faith not complete apart from ours. (Hebrews 11:39–40 TMSG)*

It takes our faith and their faith joining together to accomplish all God wants accomplished in this hour. Remember, God says that faith, hope, and love abide; therefore, their faith is still alive and we can join with their faith.

Rick Joyner wrote the following in one of his *Word for the Week* articles:

> *Negiel Bigpond is a great Native American leader, and I consider him an elder in the body of Christ. He told us that when his mother was dying, she did not just tell him that she loved him, but she told him what translated, 'If you do not do what we taught you and prepared you to do, we did not exist.' Negiel finally understood what she meant. She saw life as a river, flowing, going somewhere. If her children did not carry on the family mission, then the river stopped flowing and would soon be entirely forgotten.*

In this end-time, we must have unity with those who have gone before us just as Jesus did. He had such confidence in His life on earth because it was based upon the faith of those who went before Him. He was fulfilling their faith for a coming Savior even though they were long gone from this earth. Additionally, He was fulfilling the faith of those who would yet believe on Him even until the end of this age.

My prayer is not for them alone. I pray also for those who will believe in me through their message, that all of them may be one ... May they be brought to complete unity to let the world know that you sent me and have loved them even as you have loved me. (John 17:20–23 NIV)

Agreeing with Previous Generations

We can agree with what was released on earth in previous generations. An excellent prayer to agree with is the prayer the Israelites sung in Numbers 21:17–18. We can apply this prayerful song to the government of this country, the United States of America, to spring up. Specifically, we have the right to pray the well dug by the nation's nobles (the Founding Fathers) would spring up. By implication, praying for the well to spring up means it is not flowing as it should, or it has dried up. Because of this, we should sing and pray that the well of the Founding Fathers would flow again:

> *Spring up, O well!*
> *All of you sing to it—*
> *The well the leaders sank,*
> *Dug by the nation's nobles,*
> *By the lawgiver, with their staves.*
> *(Numbers 21:17–18)*

We can pray for God to give us Godly leaders like in the founding of our nation and for a great harvest to come forth from our nation.

Praying with Honor

God wants us to honor our fathers and our mothers. This applies to our natural and our spiritual heritage. To honor our spiritual heritage, we need to have our hearts joined with those who have labored throughout the generations. By joining with the prayers of the saints, we honor our spiritual fathers and mothers, which also honors God. Far too often, we have forgotten about those who have labored for God in past generations. This is forgetting not just them, but it is forgetting a part of God—His work through them.

For many of us, we can also join with the prayers of our fathers, mothers, and grandparents. I remember stories told to me of my ancestors praying for their future generations. My mother's side of the family is especially my spiritual heritage; they prayed for me not knowing who I would be except that I would be carrying on their work for the Lord. I am fulfilling some of the work they started years ago. What a privilege it is to know you are a part of something bigger than yourself.

My wife and I pray for our children to carry on what we have started—for God's work goes on from generation to generation. Remember, God refers to Himself as the God of Abraham, Isaac, and Jacob. He is the God of the generations; He sees His work as one continuous stream. So when you pray, realize you are where you are because of the work of God through others; thank Him for the prayers and labors of those who have gone before you. This type of prayer honors God and all His workings through others.

Prayer of Agreement

When people agree in prayer while alive on earth, their prayer causes a response from heaven. However, since prayers do not die but are alive even after a person dies, the prayer of agreement can apply to agreeing with those that have gone before us. When we see God's work is one continuous work and agree with it in prayer, it moves the hand of God.

> *When two of you get together on anything at all on earth and make a prayer of it, my Father in heaven goes into action. (Matthew 18:19 TMSG)*

The prayer of agreement is essential in this hour because when the generations from Adam to the present are joined, we will see the Lord as The First and The Last; we will see Him for who He is—The Beginning and The End, The Author and Finisher of our faith.

Praying with Thanksgiving

Have we received things from God through previous generations and never thanked Him for them? More than likely, "Yes." So let's realize we are standing on the prayers of others and be thankful for those prayers.

Also, we can pray with thanksgiving because we are living at the end of the age and will be able to fulfill the prayers of previous generations. We should not take this privilege lightly because we will see the greatest move of God ever—the greatest works, the greatest laborers, and the greatest harvest. Moreover, when the gospel of the kingdom is preached in all the world, the end will come because of the culmination of the prayers of generations.

Mature Harvest

Jesus' heart is for the harvest; He died for the harvest. In these days, an important prayer is for the harvest with plentiful laborers entering into the labors of others.

The harvest is for that which is mature, including prayers. Prayers come to maturity, or completeness—to the time of their fulfillment. Prayers from the ages gone by are now in the days of fulfillment. The saints of old as well as present believers have prayed for His kingdom to come on earth as it is in heaven, and have prayed for God to send laborers into His harvest. These prayers are now maturing—they are entering the time of fulfillment. Two-thousand years ago, Jesus told His disciples to pray for harvest laborers and thousands in history have obeyed that command. Now is the fullness of time when these prayers all come together and God will call forth the end-time harvesters—a multitude of mature laborers.

These laborers will have a mature kingdom message for the mature harvest. Why will they have a mature kingdom message? Because men and women throughout history have been faithful with their talents, and their lives are the "seed" planted that enable a harvest of end-time laborers to come forth. These laborers will honor their "fathers and mothers" that went before them, and it will take every one of these laborers to bring in this great harvest of souls.

Part Three:

THE

LABOR

Chapter 15

What Is the Labor?

B efore we go on, we want to quickly recap a few of the points of the first two sections of this book.

PART ONE: THE HARVEST

- A great harvest is at the end of the age.

- We are living at the end of the age.

- There is a great harvest in our day.

- A key to the harvest is the prayer for laborers.

PART TWO: THE PRAYER

- Prayer is experiencing relationship with God.

- Through Christ, you can approach God at any time.

- The struggle is with the flesh, not prayer.

- Pray even when God already knows the need.

- It is about God, humankind, and the great end-time harvest.

- Our prayers joined with the prayers throughout history are what God uses to bring forth the end-time harvest.

The Laborer

Since Jesus made clear the need for prayer for laborers in the harvest, men and women throughout history have prayed for God to send forth laborers. Because of this, many laborers are being prepared and sent into the great harvest of our day. This section of the book concerns the labor of those laborers—the use of their talents.

Labor Is Work

The name "laborers" is significant; it means there is work involved. In this case, it is the work of the harvest. Jesus said the harvest is great, but the laborers are few. Because of this, He commanded us to pray for God to send out laborers so that all the work of the harvest would be accomplished. Since the end-time harvest is so great, we have a heavy responsibility with much labor involved. However, labor in God's kingdom is quite different from our idea of labor.

Laboring with Jesus

Here is what Jesus said about our labor:

> ***Come to Me, all you who labor and are heavy laden, and I will give you rest. Take My yoke upon you and learn from Me, for I am gentle and lowly in heart, and you will find rest for your souls. For My yoke is easy and My burden is light. (Matthew 11:28–30)***

We accomplish our labor *with* Jesus (to be "yoked to Jesus" means to be *closely united with Him* to do the work). By being closely united with Jesus we will accomplish what needs to be done. Jesus explains this beautifully in John 15:4–8:

"Live in me, and I will live in you. A branch cannot produce any fruit by itself. It has to stay attached to the vine. In the same way, you cannot produce fruit unless you live in me.

"I am the vine. You are the branches. Those who live in me while I live in them will produce a lot of fruit. But you can't produce anything without me. . . . You give glory to my Father when you produce a lot of fruit and therefore show that you are my disciples." (GW)

We glorify God when we produce a lot of fruit. We do this by living in Christ—having His life flowing through us. God chose us to be the answer to the prayers of many saints to labor with Jesus to gather in this great end-time harvest of souls.

You didn't choose me, but I chose you. I have appointed you to go, to produce fruit that will last, and to ask the Father in my name to give you whatever you ask for. (John 15:16 GW)

Jesus chose us to labor with Him in the harvest, and as we do this, we are to ask the Father in Jesus' name for whatever we need to accomplish our work. This makes the end-time harvest sure, since Jesus chooses the laborers and the Father gives them whatever they need to bring in the harvest.

Gifted for Labor

The labor is the work it takes for us to do God's will—to use our giftings. What does this labor look like? It's the labor involved in making disciples, teaching them to obey all that Jesus taught through our giftings.

The Scriptures inform us that we all have been given gifts from God; the issue is whether we use our gifts. An expensive gift not used is an insult to the giver. If a father gives a child a new car with the title and keys but the child never uses it, showing that the gift had no value to the child, it would be insulting since it cost so much and was valued so little. Our Father in heaven may be grieved also if we do not value His gifts enough to use them when He paid the highest price for them—His Son.

God is creative and will have interesting ways of harvesting His harvest—not all of His people will harvest in exactly the same way. So, how do we reap the harvest? It is by doing whatever He commands us to do—He shows each one of us individually an aspect of our work in the harvest.

Harvesting Methods

Because it is the Lord's harvest fields, you do not harvest any way you choose. He sends us forth according to His will, His direction. Some will write books; some will publish books; some will write songs; some will sing songs; some will preach in churches; others will preach to drug addicts and prostitutes; some will harvest in the cities and others in rural areas; some will be sent to unreached people groups and others to America; some will harvest from other religions and others from atheists. God has the exclusive right to direct the harvesters since it is His harvest field.

Many only think of the evangelistic part of the harvest—getting people born again. But the harvest has many more aspects to it, and knowing what aspect of the harvest you are to fulfill is vitally important. Your "yoke" with Jesus is His giftings that He gives you to operate in.

> *Now to each one of us grace has been given according to the measure of Christ's gift. . . . some to be apostles, others to be prophets, others to be evangelists, and still others to be pastors and teachers, to perfect the saints, to do the work of ministry, and to build up the body of Christ . . . . (Ephesians 4:7–12 ISV)*

This Scripture shows us there is a 5-fold nature to His giftings. The following is an oversimplified summary of the nature of these giftings:

- Apostolic—to be sent to lay the foundation and to oversee the churches.

- Prophetic—to see and know the current and future will of God.

- Evangelistic—to bring others to faith in Christ.

- Pastoral—to care for others.

- Teaching—to instruct in the ways of Christ.

Your gifting will take on one or more of these aspects of the harvest. This does not mean that you will have the title or be in the office of one of these gifts; it means the gift(s) you have will have a nature similar to one of the 5-fold giftings.

Use YOUR Gifting

Caution! Some laborers may try to get you to labor in their callings, since that is how they see God bringing in the harvest; they do not realize God has other means of bringing in the harvest. Don't be yoked to one of the 5-fold giftings that Jesus has not yoked you to.

> *... So since we find ourselves fashioned into all these excellently formed and marvelously functioning parts in Christ's body, let's just go ahead and be what we were made to be, without enviously or pridefully comparing ourselves with each other, or trying to be something we aren't.*
>
> *If you preach, just preach God's Message, nothing else; if you help, just help, don't take over; if you teach, stick to your teaching; if you give encouraging guidance, be careful that you don't get bossy; if you're put in charge, don't manipulate; if you're called to give aid to people in distress, keep your eyes open and be quick to respond; if you work with the disadvantaged, don't let yourself get irritated with them or depressed by them. Keep a smile on your face. (Romans 12:5–8 TMSG)*

A large percentage of Christians will be laborers in whatever place they find themselves. If you are in the arts and entertainment part of society, then God will use your giftings there. You may be in the educational field, the governmental field, the media field, the religious arena, or in the family arena; wherever you are, use your talents. Remember, Jesus was still a carpenter when He was well pleasing to the Father and heard the Father's pleasure announced from heaven:

> *Then a voice came from heaven, "You are My beloved Son, in whom I am well pleased." (Mark 1:11)*

A smaller percentage of Christians' labor will be 24/7 prayer. Personally, one of my main parts in the harvest at this time is writing books for the harvest. My writing gift is an example of the pastoral and teaching aspects of His 5-fold giftings.

The harvest is not just about getting people saved; it is about bringing them into the fullness of Christ.

> *. . . until all of us are united in the faith and in the full knowledge of God's Son, and until we attain mature adulthood and the full standard of development in Christ. (Ephesians 4:13 ISV)*

We must have all five aspects of the laborers for the harvest to mature into what God desires—full development in Christ. For this purpose, we need all of the body of Christ using their giftings.

Why Teach Obedience?

Jesus said to make disciples teaching them to obey everything He commanded (Matthew 28:20). Why? First, we all have a life to live based upon what God gives us, and our life speaks louder than our words. To say it another way, your living the life of a disciple is the best teaching, for your words mean little if you are not living what you are saying. Even today, the words of Jesus are still powerful because He lived what He preached. We are to be His disciples and live what we preach or our words will have little value and we will not see much of a harvest.

Second, we need to teach obedience to Jesus because this enables us to know the One we are following. That is, doing what He says causes us to want to know the One who said these things and the more we know the One who commands these things, the more we fall in love with Him. The "obeying" simply keeps our hearts open and soft before Him, while disobedience hardens the heart. A soft heart is open to falling deeply in love.

If you keep my commands, you'll remain intimately at home in my love. That's what I've done—kept my Father's commands and made myself at home in his love. (John 15:10 TMSG)

We want to "do" for Him because we love Him. Our obedience to Him is simply the outflow of our heart of love. In fact, we will do anything for Him when we love Him fully. Our love will compel us to do what He says; we will not hide our "talent" because of our love for Him.

WHAT IS THE LABOR?   151

A primary purpose in life is to *be* a disciple. Being a disciple is more important than doing something; even so, a true disciple will do the works of a disciple.

The Harvesters

We are the harvesters that previous generations have prayed for—the answer to the past prayers of thousands. We are now in the harvest age and we are the ones who are to harvest the ripe fields. We are the answer to the prayer for laborers. We are the ones God wanted born in this time. Even so, God's plan did not start with us; it started from before the foundation of the world. Therefore, we must realize it is not just about us; we are just a part of God's eternal plan and our part is to be the harvesters that others have labored for in prayer.

Harvesting the Life

The heart of the Father at this time is the harvesting of His Son's work on the cross—the harvesting of the life released in Jesus' death on the cross. His blood planted in the earth produced a harvest of life. That harvest was immediate as well as future. There has always been a harvest since the beginning of time since Jesus was the lamb slain from before the foundation of the world; even so, the greatest harvest is at the end of the age when all things come to maturity. We are at the time of the great harvest, which is the end of the age of man's rule on the earth. That is, before Jesus comes to rule on the earth, man's rule on the earth comes to maturity.

All of creation is waiting for the revealing of the sons of God—the mature harvest of Jesus' death on the cross. Romans 8:19 says, ***"For the earnest expectation of*** *the creation eagerly waits for the revealing of the sons of God.*" These mature sons of God are mature because of all God has done throughout history. It's not just about them; it is about what God has matured throughout the generations through His Son and His Spirit. As the Scripture states, **"For we are His workmanship created in Christ Jesus for good works, which God prepared beforehand that we should walk in them"** *(Ephesians 2:10).*

The sons of God that Romans 8:19 speaks of are being matured at this time in history; soon they will be revealed to reap the harvest. And it is not unreasonable to expect to be a part of these matured sons since God is maturing a people at this time in history. Whether God ever considers us as such is His business; nevertheless, we all have our part to play in this end-time harvest; so let's do our part of the harvesting.

The Rest

Jesus has called you to bring heaven to earth just as He did—His burden is light and His yoke is easy, and you find rest for your soul. The rest is for your soul—it is not for you to do nothing. You are yoked to the Lord who is doing a great work in your day, so you will be working too. However, He will be the one empowering the work that is done. Your rest is knowing that He is carrying most of the load so your burden is light. You have work to do—to follow His leading, to go where He goes, and to do what He does. Imitate Christ! By doing this it will compel others to follow Christ and to hear those words, "Well done, good and faithful servant."

Chapter 16

Overcoming Fear

In the *Parable of the Talents*, the wicked servant hid his talent because he was afraid. Again, we emphasize the point that fear can keep us from using our talent. Specifically, a fear of rejection can cause us to hide our talent instead of using it for God's glory—His harvest.

After the death of Jesus, the disciples were hiding because of fear (see John 20:19). They were hiding because of the fear of rejection and the possibility of being physically hurt.

The Power

The disciples needed a power beyond themselves to overcome this fear. We have the same need; we need the power to overcome fear and to be the witness Jesus wants. Jesus tells us how this will happen in Acts 1:8:

> *But you shall receive power when the Holy Spirit has come upon you; and you shall be witnesses to Me in Jerusalem, and in all Judea and Samaria, and to the end of the earth.*

When those who were hiding in fear received the baptism of the Holy Spirit on the Day of Pentecost, they became bold witnesses and about three thousand people were born again that day. This is the same way we will overcome fear—by the power of the Holy Spirit.

The Fire

Fire is our friend and foe. It's warm and cozy, ferocious and scary; it draws you in, and scares you away.

After Jesus left the earth, He so loved us that He could hardly wait to come back to us in the Holy Spirit. Therefore, the Holy Spirit raced full force to His people on the Day of Pentecost—He came as a mighty rushing wind baptizing them in the fire of His love. Our God's love is a consuming fire. Nothing can consume us like His love. His Love, goodness, and kindness can truly change us (see Romans 2:4).

Let's see how the Holy Spirit came on the disciples in Acts 2:3–4:

> *They saw what seemed to be tongues of fire that separated and come to rest on each of them. All of them were filled with the Holy Spirit and began to speak in other tongues as the Spirit enabled them. (NIV)*

The "tongues of fire" indicated their ability to be His witnesses by the power of the Holy Spirit. These tongues of fire were on each one signifying we all can be witnesses by the Holy Spirit's power. These tongues of fire were *visible* because it's obvious the power is from the Holy Spirit.

John the Baptist said that Jesus would baptize us in fire. *"He will baptize you with the Holy Spirit and fire" (Matthew 3:11).* The Holy Spirit's fire casts out the fear from our mind and heart. *"For our God is a consuming fire" (Hebrews 12:29).* The fire of the

Spirit produces the fiery works in us as it did for the early disciples who had previously hid because of fear; but after they were baptized in the Spirit, they were used mightily in the harvest. And when they were threatened by men, they prayed for more boldness and received more infilling of the Spirit and preached even more boldly.

> *And now they're at it again! Take care of their threats and give your servants fearless confidence in preaching your Message, as you stretch out your hand to us in healings and miracles and wonders done in the name of your holy servant Jesus.*

> *While they were praying, the place where they were meeting trembled and shook. They were all filled with the Holy Spirit and continued to speak God's Word with fearless confidence. (Acts 4:29–31 TMSG)*

Fire the Fear

If you are afraid, it is because you are too far from The Fire. When you get close enough to The Fire, He will consume your fear, for our God *is* a consuming fire.

Fear can cause you to back away from The Fire; faith causes you to draw near to The Fire.

> *For whatever is born of God overcomes the world. And this is the victory that has overcome the world—our faith. (1 John 5:4)*

Faith in yourself will not overcome fear. Peter found this out when he vehemently proclaimed his power not to deny Jesus even though others might; but when the test came, he denied Jesus three times out of fear. Even so, when Peter was baptized in the Holy Spirit and fire, he overcame fear.

We need to pray for fire, the fire of the Holy Spirit, lest we hide our talents out of fear. Then after praying for the fire, draw near to God and He (The Fire) will draw near to you (see James 4:8).

These are the days of men's hearts failing them physically and emotionally because of fear. Luke 21:26 states:

"Men's hearts failing them from fear and the expectation of those things which are coming on the earth, for the powers of the heavens will be shaken."

We will not escape fear unless we are close to The Fire. We need to "fire" the fear with love because love is the greatest weapon against fear. The more you love God, the closer you will get to Him and this burns out fear.

There is no fear in love; but perfect love casts out fear, because fear involves torment. But he who fears has not been made perfect in love. We love Him because He first loved us. (1 John 4:18–19)

When we know that God loves us so much, we will not be tormented with the fear of Him hurting us or punishing us; but we will draw closer and closer to Him and His presence will burn out the fear.

When we are afraid, we need to realize it is because we are too far from God. I have found that the times I have been most afraid are the times I am not close enough to God—I have let the cares of this world keep me from His presence making me susceptible to fear. When this has happened, the only way I found to "fire the fear" is to draw close to The Fire—Jesus.

Jesus has eyes like a flame of fire, signifying His great love for us. When He looks at us with such great love, it melts away all fear. When we are afraid, we simply need to see His fiery love for us and watch the fear melt away.

Jesus will cause your heart to burn as He opens the Scripture to you (see Luke 24:32). "Opening the Scripture" means He gives understanding of the Word of God and when you see and understand it, your heart will burn. When The Word opens up the Scriptures for you, it causes your heart to burn for Him.

> *Do not let this Book of the Law depart from your mouth; meditate on it day and night, so that you may be careful to do everything written in it. Then you will be prosperous and successful. Have I not commanded you? Be strong and courageous. Do not be terrified; do not be discouraged, for the LORD your God will be with you wherever you go. (Joshua 1:8–9 NIV)*

As God told Joshua to be strong and of good courage and possess the inheritance, so He is telling us to use our talents and to reap the end-time harvest.

Chapter 17

Results of the Labor

O ur labor has supernatural results—it results in the completion of all of the labors that went before us.

We have stories of those who were stoned, sawed in two, murdered in cold blood; stories of vagrants wandering the earth in animal skins, homeless, friendless, powerless—the world didn't deserve them!—making their way as best they could on the cruel edges of the world.

Not one of these people, even though their lives of faith were exemplary, got their hands on what was promised. God had a better plan for us: that their faith and our faith would come together to make one completed whole, their lives of faith not complete apart from ours. (Hebrews 11:37–40 TMSG)

Wow! All of our labor will be worth it, not just for us, but for all the laborers throughout history also. We have the privilege of entering into their labor, finishing what they started. This is one of the results of our labor—finishing the labor of others.

Another result of our labor (being yoked with Jesus) is Christlikeness—to be like Jesus Christ, the Anointed One. When we are like Christ, we will be anointed and do

what He did—He went about doing good and healing all
that were oppressed by the devil.

> *Then Jesus arrived from Nazareth,*
> *anointed by God with the Holy Spirit,*
> *ready for action. He went through the*
> *country helping people and healing*
> *everyone who was beaten down by the*
> *Devil. He was able to do all this because*
> *God was with him. (Acts 10:38 TMSG)*

According to Jesus, we will do the same things He did
and even greater things (see John 14:12).

A third result of our labor will be understanding the
value of every disciple. In Acts 2, God pours out His
spirit on all His people—male and female, young and old.
We are all valuable and needed for the harvest. If you
have ever had a large project, you appreciate every hand
of help. The end-time harvest is so large that we will
appreciate every person who helps in any way.
1 Corinthians 12 shows us that each person is vitally
important; even so, He may give more talent to some;
but to whom more is given, more is required. Remember,
we are all rewarded for our labor based upon what we do
with what we are given. And as "one body," we are to
rejoice together for everyone's accomplishments.

A fourth result is to see the value of every soul. In this
harvest, God will spare no expense to save even one soul.
When we see what God does for the most unlikely ones,
we will know the value He places on saving people.
Saving souls will again be valued as it should be.

Jesus Lifted Up

A fifth result of our labor will display Jesus as the Way, the Truth, and the Life—as the Good Shepherd—as the One crucified for us. This will bring about the end result of our labor—people drawn to Jesus Christ, and becoming His disciplined followers. Jesus said it this way:

> *"As for me, if I am lifted up from the earth, I will draw all people to myself." He said this to indicate the kind of death he was about to die. (John 12:32–33 ISV)*

The end of this age will come when the gospel of the kingdom is preached in every nation (see Matthew 24:14). When we preach Christ and Him crucified, it will draw all people to Him resulting in the great end-time harvest. Multitudes will become the temple of the Holy Spirit; then Jesus will present the harvest from all of history to the Father. These will be the Father's blood-bought children He purchased with His Son's blood. The Father will then give Jesus the bride His Son has so longed for. This is great news for us as we realize that our labor plays an important part in giving God His children and Jesus His bride. What a privilege to work for such a result!

Conclusion

The phrase "Well done" is for those that do well. These ones do well because of the grace of God—our enabling to please Him. As I have heard many say, *"It takes God to love God."* So it is with serving God, obeying God, and pleasing God; we will do well only by God's grace.

We need God's grace as the Apostle Paul constantly stressed. Along with that grace, we also need the peace of God which only comes through Christ Jesus. Thus, the answer to living in peace is following Jesus—being His disciple. John 8:32 is often quoted out of context because verse 32 is vitally linked to verse 31. Let's look at verse 31 with verse 32:

> *Then Jesus said to those Jews who believed Him, "If you abide in My word, you are My disciples indeed. And you shall know the truth, and the truth shall make you free." (John 8:31–32)*

True freedom is found in being Jesus' disciple. A disciple abides in Jesus' word. A disciple *lives* according to what Jesus taught. A disciple obeys Jesus. This is the pathway to true peace and rest.

Do not strive to hear, "Well done, good and faithful servant." If you want to hear "Well done," simply obey. As we yield to the Word of God it does the surgery in our hearts for obedience. Only as we obey the Word of God can we have true peace and rest. This does not mean that we will never stumble or fall into sin. James 3:2 says, *"For we all stumble in many things."* The difference for a disciple is that they quickly repent, trust in the blood of Jesus for forgiveness, and move on. They enter into the rest of being forgiven—not trying to earn their forgiveness through what they do. They know that the blood of Jesus is enough.

> *For though a righteous man falls seven times, he rises again . . ." (Proverbs 24:16)*

Don't ever give up. You can make it to the end by Christ's strength. He is the Truth, the Life, and the Way to hear, *"Well done, good and faithful servant."* When you need help, remember Hebrews 4:16, *"Let us therefore come boldly to the throne of grace, that we may obtain mercy and find grace to help in time of need."*

God calls our yielding to Him instead of doing things our way, obedience—being a good and faithful servant. For this reason, our response to Him is of critical importance to our hearing, *"Well done."*

Jesus knows all of the possible responses to His Word and their results. He tells us in the *Parable of the Sower* that it will be one of these responses:

> *". . . I tell stories: to create readiness, to nudge the people toward receptive insight. . . .*
>
> *"Study this story of the farmer planting seed. When anyone hears news of the kingdom and doesn't take it in, it just remains on the surface, and so the Evil*

One comes along and plucks it right out of that person's heart. This is the seed the farmer scatters on the road.

"The seed cast in the gravel—this is the person who hears and instantly responds with enthusiasm. But there is no soil of character, and so when the emotions wear off and some difficulty arrives, there is nothing to show for it.

"The seed cast in the weeds is the person who hears the kingdom news, but weeds of worry and illusions about getting more and wanting everything under the sun strangle what was heard, and nothing comes of it.

"The seed cast on good earth is the person who hears and takes in the News, and then produces a harvest beyond his wildest dreams." (Matthew 13:13–23 TMSG)

To the one who produces a harvest, Jesus will say:

"Well Done!"

Author Steven J. Campbell may be contacted at his personal email:

stevecamp3@hotmail.com

Or on Facebook:

www.facebook.com/StevenJCampbellBooks

The Christian's Bill of Rights
A 31-Day Devotional to Help You Live Free
by Steven J. Campbell

This book can help you live in the hope and
freedom Jesus purchased for you on the cross.

WELL DONE

GOOD AND FAITHFUL SERVANT

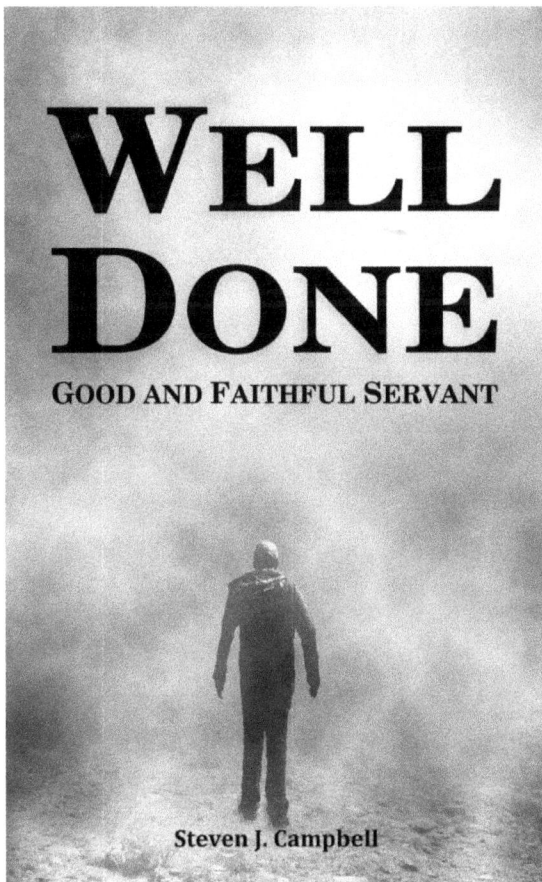

Steven J. Campbell

Well Done:
Good and Faithful Servant
by Steven J. Campbell

This book is for helping you fulfill your purpose in the end-time harvest and to hear Jesus say, "Well done."

Steven J. Campbell

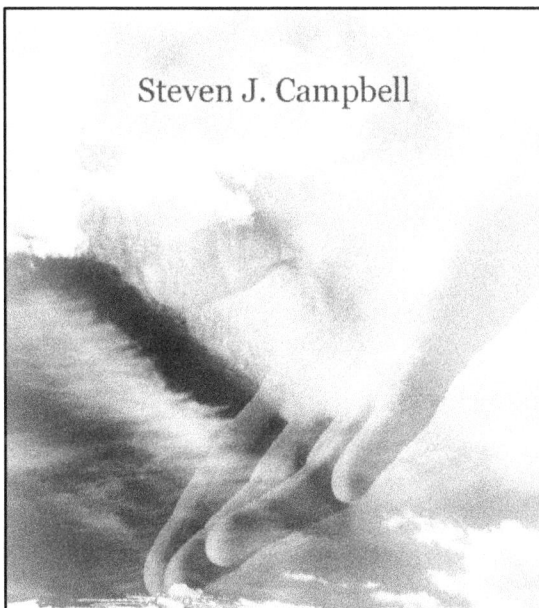

I AM BORN AGAIN,
NOW WHAT?

An Invitation to Grow in Christ

I AM BORN AGAIN, NOW WHAT?
An Invitation to Grow in Christ

by Steven J. Campbell
and
Austin J. Campbell

This book is about growing in Christ in the basics of Christianity, experiencing His love in a greater measure.

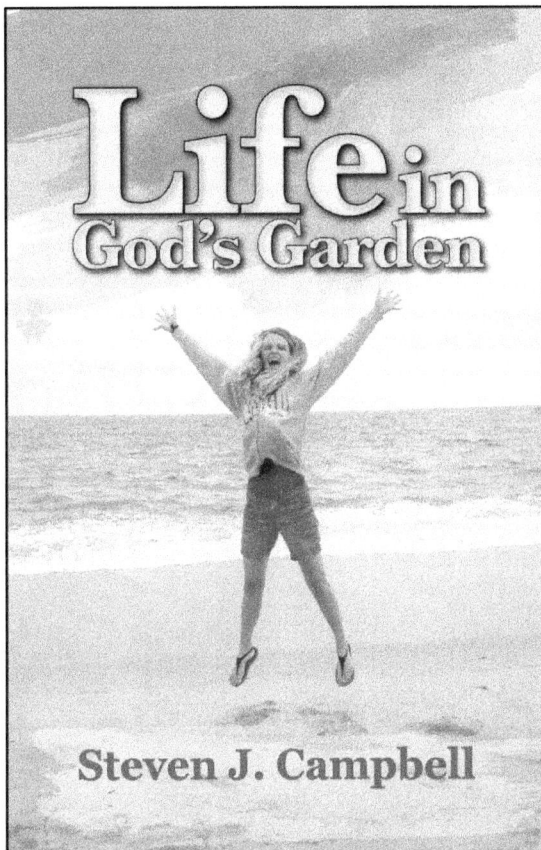

Life in God's Garden
by Steven J. Campbell
and
Austin J. Campbell

This book is about important principles found in the Garden of Eden. By understanding these, it helps you live as the Lord's special garden.

God Revealed
His Revelation to Us
Steven J. Campbell
Austin J. Campbell   Isaiah X.A. Begay

Foreword by
Christie DeWees

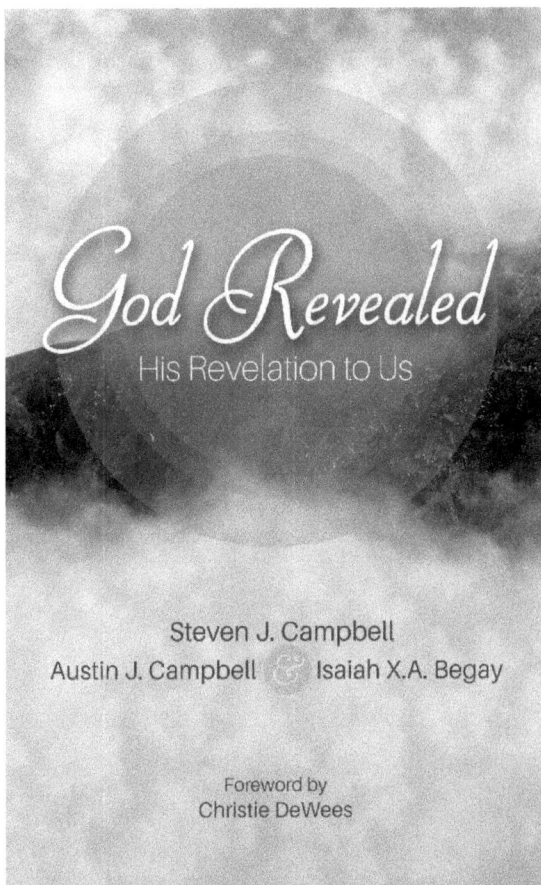

God Revealed
His Revelation to Us
*by Steven J. Campbell,
Austin J. Campbell,
and Isaiah X.A. Begay*

*God reveals Himself in the Scriptures. Join us
in mining the deep mysteries of God, finding
the most valuable treasure—His essence.*

www.ingramcontent.com/pod-product-compliance
Lightning Source LLC
Chambersburg PA
CBHW071053040426
42443CB00013B/3319